Dearest Le...

I hope this
increase the enthusiasm
you certainly already
do have.

With love, Ross
Xmas 1983

Vital Enthusiasm

James E. Melton, Ph.D.

Global Publications
P.O. Box 2112 • Palm Springs, California 92263

Acknowledgement

In a world that is doing its best to try to make you just like everyone else, it is, indeed, rare to find someone who has dedicated his life toward helping others achieve individuality and self expression. However trite, the truth still remains that we teach best by example. In addition, it is also true that through devoted guidance, we may become the catalyst to accelerate the learning process of another beyond a point which may not have appeared as realistic.

This guidance I speak of must be acknowledged from another point of view, and that is the willingness of the recipient to seek a better way. Behind every successful person stands an individual who provided the impetus for success. It pleases me greatly that I have reached the point in my life whereby I allowed myself the privilege of benefiting from the wisdom and guidance of one so gifted as my tutor, counselor and friend, Dr. James L. Ross, whom I reverently call "Wizard." This type of relationship was the foundation upon which the following personal success plan was based. I wish the reader every success based upon my book, but even more, I wish you your own Dr. Ross.

To Wizard

CONTENTS

CONTENTS

Introduction

To be successful in one's own terms, whether in business or personal life, requires techniques that are effectively tailored for a specific task at hand. The Personal Success Plan presented in this book offers guidelines intended to enhance the personal development of every individual. The basic premise is that the more an individual becomes aware and uses his potential, the greater his quality of life. Thus, both individuals and corporations can benefit by exerting a more positive influence on those surrounding them.

Many writers have offered crash programs designed to, in one way or another, improve the individual. This author makes no such claims because his personal experience suggests that any benefits gained from such programs are usually short-lived. In this new book, the reader is provided a step-by-step, 90-day program designed to permanently alter his

Introduction

life-style in a positive direction. This guided plan for success offers each individual the opportunity to observe, evaluate and design his own growth for application in all facets of life.

The reader might question the use of an apple for the book cover. Apples are closely associated with teachers, students, well-being and health. By the end of this book, you can become both teacher and student. Remember, "an apple a day will keep the negatives away." Now, take the first bite.

James E. Melton, Ph.D.

1

A Positive Direction

1

A Positive Direction

For the most part it has been the policy of businesses to seek out and to acquire the talents of the most qualified persons in the field and then train them for a specific task. The major emphasis has been on technical data specifically directed at the particular firm in which those talents are to be administered. Once this training process has been accomplished, the individual is essentially thrust into the practical arena to, figuratively speaking, live or die, with only an occasional meaningful contact from the sales manager or general director.

Relatively little regard is offered to this individual in relation to his capacity for psychological adjustment to his new position, and virtually nothing is done to instill in him a permanent attitude toward personal motivation. If the individual fares well, his success can be seen as being directly related to his innate capacity for self-direction, persistence and motivation. The natural extension of this success phenomenon is appropriately stated by Peter and Hull: "In a hierachy, every employee tends to rise to his level of incompetence."[1]

Corporate society has become more technologically oriented, yet for the most part, the individual, who is the real foundation of corporate strength, has been often and curiously ignored. Self-direction and persistence are natural by-products of motivation. When a task is initiated, the need to organize becomes evident as a means toward realizing a viable end. Here the technical advice of the hiring firm is helpful in guiding the individual into areas that will enhance productivity. Persistence to continue is present, even in the face of adversity, in one who has an inner motivation, because whatever the reason, the desire to achieve is of prime importance to the individual. Motivation, then, whether in one's personal life or in business, is a key ingredient to success of any lasting nature.

Readily apparent, owing to the widespread use of business-related motivational seminars and the numerous writings on the subject, is that businesses want to isolate a quality within the employee that effectively deals with motivation on an internal level. Individual programs such as EST, Mind Control, Life Spring, and writings tailored toward enhancing corporate efficiency, i.e., *I'm OK, You're OK, Up the Organization* and *Working Smart*, all make a viable attempt at releasing individual potential for expression in job-related tasks, but somehow, in each one the longevity of this quality is eluded. This writer acknowledges the myriad of research on motivation, but quarrels with the application of, and the lack of personal involvement in, applications to results orientation.

To relate this hypothesis, this researcher questions whether there exists a long-term effect through present-day motivational techniques, and if one does exist, in this writer's opinion, there seems to be no research available to correlate the long-term success of existing programs. The term "success" is one which has many meanings depending upon individual perception. For the purpose of this writing, the word success means:

The continuing, constructive evolvement of an individual toward a positive outcome, which is accomplished by using internal means directed to both personal and business endeavors.

With this in mind, it would seem that a beneficial area of exploration for business would be the area of personal motivation with long-lasting results. A reliable process that would stimulate objectiveness, enhance visionary capabilities, and influence self-induced productivity would most certainly be a desirable asset. Unlocking a motivational force for individual expression and directing this vital energy into specific areas of life in a permanent and self-guided fashion would be most challenging and rewarding.

Every person seemingly has a built-in desire to fan into flame that spark deep within himself. But what is it that drives some forward while others remain status quo? Could it be that some connect their daydreams, their aspirations and their fantasies to their work world while others do not?

There is sufficient data available to know how to effectively transform failure into success, debt into profit, and work into enjoyment. There is no veil of mystery, just clear practical laws to be properly developed and systematically applied. Countless studies have proved the positive link between vivid mental imagery and actual physical accomplishment — what this writer has termed "Vital Enthusiasm." Why not use this to create a more positive thought atmosphere, thereby resulting in action-oriented behavior? Also, it is known that individual needs for achievement can be measured; they are directly related to people who have a habitual thinking pattern toward improvement.[2] This pattern is learned. The evidence suggests that it is not because individuals are born that way, but because of special training they received in the home from parents who set moderately high achievement goals and who tended to be warm, encouraging and non-authoritarian in helping their children reach these goals.

Webster's dictionary defines motivation as: "furnishing with a motive or motives; to give impetus to; to incite; to impel."[3] Again, Webster's defines vital as: "being concerned with, or manifesting of life, and essential to the existence or continuance of something." It also describes enthusiasm as: "being inspired; intense or eager interest; zeal."[4] Linking these together with the interpretation of success, the words Vital Enthusiasm most clearly fulfill the needs of this writing. The awakening of Vital Enthusiasm within an individual would, therefore, automatically ensure the end result long sought by businesses. Achieving results in this area through a direct and straightforward fashion would seem to be the area necessary to explore and develop at the onset of initiating, restructuring or expanding any business. While the main premise herein has direct application to the business milieu, every individual can apply the precepts successfully to his life. Therefore, a reliable method of achieving direct results in Vital Enthusiasm for personal expression is the reason for this investigation.

Questions

For this investigation to be complete and to be considered valid, the following questions are posed:

1. What activates Vital Enthusiasm?
   See . . . INNER QUALITIES and
            OUTER CONDITIONING

2. Can Vital Enthusiasm be achieved through training?
   See . . . ACQUIRING SKILLS

3. Under what conditions does the individual maximize potential using Vital Enthusiasm?
   See . . . PERSONAL SUCCESS PLAN, (PSP)

4. Can the expectant success factor of Vital Enthusiasm be determined and measured?
   See . . . THE EVALUATION PROCESS

A Positive Direction

[1]Dr. Laurence J. Peter and Raymond Hull, *The Peter Principle* (New York: Bantam Books, 1970), p. 7.

[2]Kolb, Rubin, McIntyre, *Organizational Psychology* A Book of Readings, 2nd ed. (New Jersey: Prentice Hall, Inc., 1974), p. 148-149.

[3]*Webster's New Twentieth Century Dictionary* Unabridged, 2nd ed. (Wm. Collins Pub. Inc., 1979), p. 1173.

[4]*Webster's New Twentieth Century Dictionary* Unabridged, 2nd ed. (Wm. Collins Pub. Inc., 1979), p. 1173.

11

Inner Qualities

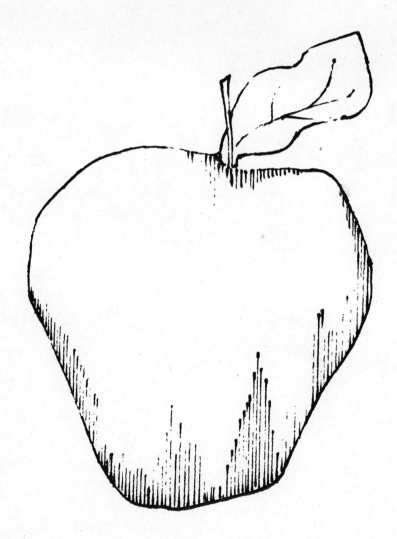

Inner Qualities

Strong reference has been made to the term Vital Enthusiasm, which is defined in this writing as: vibrance, resulting in intense, constructive and positive action. Without delving fully into the total acquisition and application of Vital Enthusiasm, some preliminary areas that tend to provide the psychic make-up of an individual will be presented. The list is not meant to be all-inclusive, but it does contain some of the inner qualities that will, with direction, assist in the long-term expression of Vital Enthusiasm.

Self-Esteem

Self-esteem may be gained through the proper development of self-image. To acknowledge that one possesses positive qualities is half the battle. It ties clearly with self-image since achievement on a "take charge" basis produces a high self-esteem. It results in freeing inherent qualities so necessary for positive achievement. Through a lack of self-awareness, individuals often misguide themselves and prevent achievement capabilities with an "I can't do it" attitude.

It has been said that, "Discovery of the self-image represents a breakthrough in psychology and the field of creative personality."[5] Observations by many, including noted psychologists, indicate that learning takes place most effectively when the student becomes free-thinking, and the self-actualizing process is most likely to release this spontaneity.[6] Thus, by raising one's self-esteem, and involving oneself with endeavors that are, by nature, inner directed, an experiential process of learning could ensue.

Learning by experience is not generally forgotten. Many believe it to be the most effective type of learning.[7] What follows, then if this type of situation is desired, the most efficient method possible to cause this process to unfold must be pursued. Raising one's self-esteem is a fundamental point, a base point foundation from which to experience life more fully.

Self-image is basically how one views himself. This sounds simple, but in reality many people are governed largely by how others view them.[8] This erroneous concept often stems from one's early years of training. Here, training is not meant to be interpreted in any sense other than actual life behavior training. Through behavior modification we learn how others feel we should conduct ourselves.[9]

Parents, although intentions are often well-meaning, will give messages opposite than intended to the child. An example would be a mother who wants her child to express the fullness of life, wants him to be creative and fun-loving; she wants for him what all loving parents want for their children. What does she do? What message does she give? Often she will be all-giving, all-sacrificing; she will often pass up opportunities to have her own good time for the sake of her children. She presents a pattern of a mothering image to her child that you must give up happiness for other people and that, at any expense, other people must be pleased. The message is that, "Other people are more important than I am."

One must realize that self-image is developed directly by the self and not by what others think or do. What seems prevalent is that one's present response to life is developed by one's own thinking. Like it or not, personal reality and experiences in life are a direct result of the choices that have been made up to the present moment.[10] When an idea or image is impressed in the mind, one tends to respond to this in the outer expression. Carrying a low opinion of oneself will tend to cause others to respond in a similar fashion. The body seems to respond to the thinking process, not only with relation to inner feelings, but also to the physical world as well.

In an experiment, U.S. Olympic Ski Team members were asked, in a classroom setting, to visualize themselves skiing down certain slopes. They were to do this with all the feelings of confidence and skill they could muster up. The findings suggest that positive classroom visualizations were directly related to improved performance on the slopes.[11]

Another experiment[12] was done at the University of Wisconsin taking three groups of people and asking them to shoot baskets on the basketball court. They were all scored. The first group was asked to practice for 20 minutes a day and return in one week to be scored. The second group was asked not to practice and return in one week to be scored. The third group was asked not to practice physically, but instead to spend 20 minutes a day, imagining that they were throwing the ball at the goal. When they missed they were to imagine that they corrected their aim accordingly. They were also asked to return in one week to be scored.

The first group, which had actually practiced 20 minutes every day, improved in scoring 24 percent.

The second group, which had no sort of practice, showed no improvement.

The third group, which practiced only in imagination, improved in scoring 23 percent.

What becomes obvious is that images, both positive and negative, that are placed in the mind affect behavior both mentally and physically. That impressions are formed at an early age is an accepted fact. Equally true is that one will tend to continue with these patterns of thinking and formulate adjusted patterns of thought only when new situations are encountered.[13] Would it not follow that when one begins employment, images begin to form in the mind relative to expected performance and, thus, one performs accordingly? This behavior pattern, developed in early business life, could affect later encounters with other firms, in either a positive or negative manner.

By impressing the mind with an image, the mind responds to the impression. There is no distinguishable difference between an actual physical image or an imaginative mental picture.[14] Implanting a desire of a favorable nature, goals, dreams and the like could be most effective and could enhance the self-image. Since the mind cannot distinguish between physical or mental impressions, the benefits of imagery are many and varied. Health maintenance and visualization go hand-in-hand to develop self-esteem. (How the area of health relates to imagery is covered in a later chapter.)

Image Barriers in Business

In many modern organizations, the manager's own ego needs account for much of his failure. An improper image held by a manager of a successful manager is most likely an underlying cause. When a manager gives his subordinates the impression that he does not care for their interests, that he is in the position of authority and he is going to rule, this creates barriers and non-productive employee attitudes.[15]

The picture of oneself as a failure is that which makes one fail.[16] To change self-image, one must create the mental image of former best achievements and project them through imagery into playing new roles that are within the scope of imagination and comprehension.

An individual's self-image is displayed at all times for all to see. Individual body language communicates to the whole world whether the individual is positive or negative. The way an individual walks, talks, the books read or not read, peer group relationships and personal interests all tell a story about an individual's self-image. Many proven methods are available for learning to communicate a positive self-image in a professional manner.[17]

In summary, the way an individual views himself is the way he greets the world; and that is exactly the way the world will greet him back. Of paramount importance is that individuals must create positive views of themselves, e.g., creative, fun-loving, spontaneous and adventuresome. Forming such mental pictures is a positive beginning to directing oneself toward greater expression and the tapping of one's inner potential. Positive self-image is, thus, a major ingredient in releasing Vital Enthusiasm.

Desire

Desire is the springboard to all achievement; the foundation on which goal realization is based. Anything that is truly desired is ultimately possible to achieve. All that needs to be done is to discover the most effective method to bring it to reality. Boldly stated, one would probably not even deeply desire something if it were not possible to achieve. Desire for anything is backed with the faith that it can be accomplished.

A belief that something is attainable will assist in developing persistence until the reality is realized. With true desire the mind is sparked to act out that which was formerly but a dream. Desire is the fire of the emotion which causes action; it can spark creative awareness of the mind. Coupled with intense desire is Vital Enthusiasm. This positively directed force recognizes no thought as impossible and accepts no failure as being a reality. Again, closely aligned with achievement, be it a physical goal, mental attunement, or career status, is self-image as an underlying factor of success.

Basic needs must be met before one rises to great achievements.[18] The physiological needs of hunger, thirst, procreation, secured shelter, and the psychological needs of social acceptance, love and self-esteem, all provide a foundation for one to act. Unless the basic needs are met, the foundation on which self-esteem is built will not be stable.

One may have high self-regard, but if cold and hungry, the desire for achievement shifts from climbing the corporate ladder to, for instance, securing food and shelter. Thus, one can clearly see the continual rise and ebb of an individual's need cycle. One may strive to reach out for a stated aim, but continually fall back due to an area needing attention. For the unaware person, this often takes place on a daily basis.

Desire is common to all and is always employed in one's natural progression toward self-fulfillment. A proper understanding of desire, provides for a more rapid development of same. Desire, from the Latin word "desyre," means from the father or source.[19] A reasonable interpretation, then, is that which is of feeling. "Desire for anything is the thing itself in incipiency."[20]

Where is the beginning? What causes one to

aspire toward advancement of any kind, be it management, sales or the executive position? Further, what brings this desire into being so that the reality may be personally experienced? Job creation, as it is defined in this writing, is both challenging and elusive and, for the most part, not generally practiced by those bucking the corporate line. Some basic points are outlined here, allowing one to avail himself of primary steps in creating a successful job position, or in enhancing the present one.

Risk-Taking

Those people who manage to sift through all the things that are handed them in life, and in spite of it manage to become guided by their own sense of purpose and direction, are known to take risks. Such risk-takers invariably do better than most in common payoffs such as prestige, income, family life, job security, etc.[11] It appears that an above average degree of risk taking emanates from those who live life for the present moment. Bending the rules by not stopping fully at a stop sign in the middle of the desert with visibility at 50 miles would not seem to be a major problem. Nor would it seem to be much of a risk. A corollary is: the greater the risk, the greater the opportunity for growth or (failure).

This is not to advocate a hit-and-miss policy, or a by-chance-alone life-style, but it does appear that most people today are tiptoeing through life carefully making their way to death. The subject here is Vital Enthusiasm, and the inner-quality of risk-taking more fully expresses it. Many people really want more out of life but are unwilling to give up their present life-style and mental attitudes; thus tomorrow becomes but an expression of today.

Most people will wake up tomorrow thinking about the problems of yesterday. If one were to continuously monitor the mind, it would reveal that about 85 percent of one's thinking is carried over into the next day. People tend to look toward tomorrow but they continually carry over many yesterdays. It's like driving an automobile: the tire blows and it is replaced. The old one is put in the trunk. Then a fender falls off and is strapped onto the automobile directly over the new one. A muffler goes bad, the new one is installed and the old one is tied right next to it. Sounds silly doesn't it? Yet most people carry forward their thoughts of guilt, envy, self-defeating behavior, sickness and anxieties into the new day without ever considering the possiblity of dropping them in the present moment and moving ahead.

A burden lifted can be a dream come true. An automobile can be streamlined by removing all the air-catching surfaces and dumping the "old stuff." So the mind can be streamlined by getting rid of some of the thoughts that tie one negatively to the past. Some people say it is too risky: "What will *they* think?" When one knows who and what they are, then what others think is not an important factor. In no way is this meant to suggest an abusive attitude or an uncaring approach to others. Simply stated, take charge with all the courage that can be mustered up and strike out with a winning attitude. Sure there will be setbacks. Of course there will be times of despair. This is all part of a master plan, without

Inner Qualities

which guidance and direction cannot effectively or rapidly move one through to predetermined and/or stated goals. We either move forward into growth, or step backward into sameness.

To be a risk-taker, one must be reasonably self-confident or the fear aspect will become overpowering. Persistence can be tiring, and wanting to achieve anything for a long period of time without action will set the tone for an unwanted habit pattern. Such a pattern will also sometimes become demoralizing to the point where the "sour grapes" attitude can be adopted. Decisiveness is extremely important, for with such action one moves forth on a path, right or wrong, to realize an immediate result. If right, the journey is continued. If wrong, a slight backtrack becomes necessary. But the fact remains that a forward move was made and it tends to lift the spirit and new directions can be planned. It has been said that Thomas Edison discovered about 16,000 different ways how *not* to make an electric light bulb. He knew where not to trod again, and each time he was more clearly set on track.

Some people go out of their way to avoid situations in which it may prove necessary or desirable to take a chance. Others seem to thrive on risk and actively seek out situations in which it may pay to gamble. It may be that the most effective decisions are made by people who are ranked neither extremely high nor extremely low in willingness to take risks. A decision-maker who is known to take large risks may fail to observe the alternative courses of action, and may end up choosing alternatives which are too risky. Conversely, a decision-maker who is overly concerned with risk-avoidance is apt to be too concerned with the evaluation process and, will have great difficulty with the final commitment. However, the decision reached may prove to be too conservative. It is the individual with an optimum willingness to take risks who knows when to continue the screening of alternatives and when to stop; when to pursue a relatively risky course and when to avoid it; who is likely to prove most effective.[22]

The decision to become a risk-taker may have to be dealt with in advance of moving forward to a more productive life-style. But move ahead one must. A risk is something which carries with it a variable amount of uncertainty. One never knows for certain just what lies ahead when any given risk is taken. Nonetheless, risks are what must be taken when any advancements are to be made, either technologically or in personality developments. Those individuals who are unwilling to give up what they presently have, or what they are comfortable with, will have the life of sameness, i.e., simply "exist" their lives away. There is nothing wrong with this as long as it fits in with one's aspirations. If it does not, which is more often the case, one must step ahead, even if ever so slightly, to experience what he thinks awaits him in the unknown and uncertain future. To never have tried is to feel remorse, but to have at least tried brings pleasure and hope for the future.

Decisiveness

Indecision is crippling; it is better to make a wrong decision than to make none at all. Life is full of decisions: what to wear, what to eat, when to move, what about marriage? All are questions; none can be answered without making a decision. Most people are really quite good at making decisions, especially when they think it is a small one. However, what is small to one may not be small to another. One may be good at making decisions for others, but fearful of deciding the course of his own life. Of note is that it is usually easier to tell others what is right for them than to take one's own advice.

A good self-image goes hand-in-hand with a good decision. As previously discussed, self-image refers to the set of feelings that people have about how they look in their own eyes and in the eyes of others. People with a positive self-concept image tend to have greater self-esteem and self-acceptance, and tend to be less anxious about what others think of them than those with a more negative view of themselves.

A self-concept image may influence descision-making effectiveness in two related ways. First, individuals with a relatively negative self-concept image will, generally, experience greater anxiety than those who think more positively of themselves. This anxiety could lead to a state of stress, making the search for, and evaluation of, alternatives extremely unlikely. Second, because of their greater concern about how they look in the eyes of others, decision-makers with a relatively negative self-concept image may be unduly sensitive to social pressure: instead of doing what they believe to be right, they may find themselves doing what they believe *others* believe as right. For both these reasons, individuals with a positive view of themselves are more likely to make effective decisions than those with negative self-concept images.[23]

[5]Maxwell Maltz, *Psycho-Cybernetics* (New York: Essandess Spedial Edition, 1960), p. v.

[6]Carl Rogers, *On Becoming A Person* (Boston: Houghton Mifflin Co., 1961), p. 285.

[7]Albert Einstein, *Out Of My Later Years* (New York: Philosophical Library, 1950), p. 32.

[8]Wayne Dyer, *Your Erroneous Zones* (New York: Funk & Wagnalls, 1976), p. 31.

[9]Thomas Harris, *I'm OK — Your OK* (New York: Harper & Row, 1967), p. 17.

[10]Joseph Murphy, *The Power of Your Subconscious Mind* (New Jersey: Prentice-Hall, Inc. 1963), p. 68.

[11]Richard Swinn, *Visual Motor Behavior Rehearsal, VMBR* research paper (Colorado: University of Colorado, Fort Collins, 1973).

[12]Maxwell Maltz, *Psycho-Cybernetics* (New York: Essandess Special Edition, 1960), p. 32.

[13]Kolb, Rubin, McIntire, *Organizational Psychology* A Book of Readings (New Jersey: Prentice Hall, 1974), p. 33.

[14]Maxwell Maltz, *Psycho-Cybernetics* (New York: Essandess Special Edition, 1960), p. 311.

[15]Bormann, Howell, Nichols, Shapiro *Interpersonal Communication in the Modern Organization* (New Jersey: Prentice-Hall, Inc. 1969), p. 151.

[16]Maxwell Maltz, *The Magic Power of Self-Image Psychology* (New York: Pocket Books, 1964), p. 59.

[17]John McCarthy, *Why Managers Fail* (New York: McGraw-Hill Pub. Co., 1978), p. 130.

DECISIVENESS

[18]Hampton, Summer, and Webber, *Organizational Behavior and the Practice of Management* (Illinois: Scott, Foresman, and Co., 1973), p. 7-10.

[19]*The Oxford Universal Dictionary* (London: Oxford at the Claredon Press, 1933), p. 457, 490, 1902.

[20]Ernest Holmes, *The Science of Mind* (New York: Dodd, Mead and Co., 1938), p. 584.

[21]Wayne Dyer, *Pulling Your Own Strings* (New York: Funk & Wagnalls-Thomas Y. Crowell Co., 1978), p. 140.

[22]Jeffery Rubin, *Making Decisions* (Reading, Massachusetts: Addison-Wesley Pub. Co., 1978), p. 68.

[23]Jeffery Rubin, *Making Decisions* (Reading, Massachusetts: Addison-Wesley Pub. Co., 1978), p. 67.

III

Outer Conditioning

Outer Conditioning

Upon first observation, one would assume that Vital Enthusiasm could best be defined as developmental assistance from an external source, possibly someone/something exerting strong influence over an individual's life. Although the part portrayed by a business manager, a spouse, a parent or a friend may be instrumental in moving or awakening the Vital Enthusiasm within an individual, the closeness of family ties seems to serve only as a mild catalyst for this development.

In general, the closer one becomes to another individual, the less apt that individual can exert influence upon him. To clarify this point, the more charisma an individual enjoys, the more likelihood of his ability to influence others. The converse is also true. Relationships of a close nature appear not as apt to stimulate rapid release of Vital Enthusiasm as would an encounter with a person removed from the individual's immediate general environment. A total stranger who passes only briefly through one's life can effectuate the decision to act; an entertainer, politician or any other external figure can be the stimulus needed. One may be impressed and startled into action by unfamiliar concepts, or even infatuated into action.

Any attempt to deliberately seek out a person who can develop Vital Enthusiasm within an individual seems unlikely. Through unawareness, one may overlook an obviously valuable source such as his teacher. One needs to examine what transpires within himself that any stranger, any removed or unknown personality, can become the needed catalyst. What prepares the individual for this event?

CATALYST COMPARISON and IMPACT FACTORS

Internal Sources	External Sources
Familiar person Friend, relative, loved one	Unfamiliar person Stranger, unknown individual.
Uses words couched in familiar framework.	Words and actions interesting because they are unfamiliar.
No need to act on ideas immediately, the person will be around for a while.	Urgency to act, the person may not pass this way again.
Considered "one of the boys."	Upper elite echelon status. Personality.
Neighborhood companion.	Expert, a long way from home.
Biased with preconceived ideas about the individual.	Unbiased, no preconceived ideas about the individual.

(Figure 1)

From the chart above, observe the many reasons an individual would sit up and take notice from an

external source, i.e., someone who is not in one's immediate environment. Bringing in an outsider can make a greater impact in shaking loose old habit patterns and ways of thinking and, in general, such individuals are greater catalysts than are close friends.

Although it appears extremely difficult, other than through blind faith or enticement, for one closely related to another to make such an impact, to cause change or to effectuate the release of Vital Enthusiasm, it can be done and has been previously accomplished. Some areas to consider for such an accomplishment are: 1. Using negative factors to develop motivation; 2. Using negative factors to build Vital Enthusiasm, and; 3. Creating models as guidelines.

Negative Reinforcement

Reverse psychology is an approach available to one when the intent is to assist one to move forward to achieve greater accomplishments. Generally, guidance is positive, but using negative statements can also be helpful. Examples are:

> "Do you think you can do it?"
> "Do you believe I can put my trust in you?"
> "I'll bet you can't do this."
> "You'll never be able to do that."
> "Many have tried before but they've always
>   failed."
> "You know better than that; it simply can't be
>   done!"

Outer Conditioning

Statements of this type arouse an, "I'll show 'em" attitude, and although the effect is usually short-term, such an attitude can be a catalyst for action-orientation.

An "I message"[24] is an implication of disapproval and will generally act as a catalyst for action, either positive or negative. If a situation is developing and calls for corrective action to be taken by someone else, but is not being done, then utilize an "I message." In short, an "I message" is a brief description of a certain behavior with one's own feelings being revealed about that behavior. Some examples are:

> "When you don't look me in the eye during our conversations . . . I feel like you are lying to me."

> "When you walk with your shoulders slumped over and looking like you are on death's doorstep . . . I feel like walking fifteen feet behind you."

> "When you don't get these letters completed on time . . . I feel like you are not concerned about my customers."

> "When you people act in this manner . . . I feel the effort we have put into this project up to this point has all been in vain."

More often than not, the result of an "I message" is that the behavior becomes adjusted, to some degree, resulting in a more desirable status.

This is not advice giving, for no advice has been offered. Far too often, one tries to correct

another's behavior by offering advice, which in most cases is not well-accepted. Sagging self-esteem and ego account for this phenomenon. Generally, people like to discover their own answers, thus building their own self-esteem.

Enticement

Although enticement does not really fall in the category of negative reinforcement, it is often associated with luring one to do something against his will. However, enticement can be both positive and negative. Painting a beautiful mental picture to essentially lure one into a situation can be accomplished for either good or bad intentions. Someone interested in another's well-being and being cognizant of the general plan of action, will often entice that individual to pursue a particular course. If clear and true, the future picture can be of great assistance in reaching a goal by being of assistance in the visualization process. Often the conveyance of such a message becomes more than just visual, and generally involves all of one's senses. When such a situation is created, the mind can be pursuaded toward some given end rather easily, since people tend to move and take action based upon feelings rather than upon intellectualization.

By allowing an individual to consider options and come to his own conclusions, the end result will usually be of a more permanent nature. Whenever something is forced, it causes strain — either in the situation or in the relationship. Doubts will arise if the enticers intentions are not of a sincere nature,

and strain and hardship may result. Nonetheless, when properly used, enticement can be an effective tool for establishing a new direction for someone. When guided by intelligence and compassion, it can be both a powerful and positive motivating force.

There is a potential problem that arises when someone attempts to assist another for his greater good. Such a problem relates to the area of responsibility. When someone is lured out of his normal, comfortable or uncomfortable environment, responsibility for behavior and actions shifts slightly. This is, in reality, only a psychological shift, such as a student/teacher or child/parent relationship. In attempting to assist, the enticer must maintain an area of control and guidance until the learner has developed confidence in his behavior and actions. At this stage of development, responsibility shifts from the teacher to the learner. This responsibility shift must be encouraged, for if the enticer continues to shoulder the burden of responsibility for any great length of time, a false sense of security is created and the strength to handle new challenges is not developed by the learner. In reality, everyone is responsible for his own life, and although outside conditioning is possible, one must be alert to other options. An individual must allow only those people whom he knows to have his best interests at heart to take part in his redirectional process.

Recognition

The need for recognition falls into a similar category of other self-defeating behaviors. At times,

when one has low self-esteem, he will let others govern him to gain recognition. The task becomes not so much that of individual endeavor, but rather of forced accomplishment to please another for an ulterior motive. In such instances, the expression of dedication would most likely be short-term. Gaining recognition by allowing others to govern one's life falls into the realm of being a puppet; it does not allow for creative thinking nor the building of self-esteem.

The reverse, however, is also true. Recognition can be a positive factor for motivation as well, and as such, the tendency for long-term positive influence may be greater. Recognition for a job well done is, indeed, a motivating force, often beyond that of money. If a high status position is maintained, much psychic income will be derived from this recognition. Congratulations, accolades and applause are what many strive for, yet rarely does one achieve what is felt to be his due commendation. Much of the so-called "deadwood" in an organization, or in a household, that cannot be understood in terms of wages, working conditions or ability, can be explained by low group or peer status. These unfortunate individuals view their situation as hopeless; they see no reason to take part or produce since they will never be regarded as valued or important people.

Reversing a Negative

The mere fact of not wanting to be like someone else is also sufficient cause to initiate change. Distrust, dislike, or simply not wishing to cultivate a close relationship with another can create the emotional impetus to move into action. Moreover, the very fact that someone of prominence does not take an interest in another may stimulate one to reach out for alternative higher achievements. The process of turning a negative into a positive applies beyond the individual. The fact that a person, a situation or a system has been functioning in a particular way for a number of weeks, months or years doesn't necessarily mean that it is the most desirable way to continue. A person, situation or system has a tendency to go on running by its own momentum, yet the longer a characteristic or process has been expressed or used, the more need there is to examine it critically.

In business, a manager is paid to find and define the problem, analyze it, develop alternate solutions, decide upon the best solution, and convert the decision into effective action.[25] Such is the nature of reversing negatives. As such, a reasonable question to start with is, "Is there a more effective way to deal with the situation?" Look for the weak spot; it may not be necessary to totally reconstruct a relationship, a situation or system, but just to cure the weak or problem areas. The most critical aspect of reversing negatives is commonality of agreement that a potentially better way exists. Without such agreement, negatives will simply remain negatives and can never be turned into positives.

Modeling

"The only rational way of educating is to be an

example."[26] To expect someone to do that which is said, and not that which is done, is not sensible. People tend to follow in the footsteps of others and, only to a lesser degree, their verbal commands. Modeling, then, is probably one of the most effective ways of teaching. Although a difficult task, it presents an effective guideline for one to learn from and follow. Just as a child learns to speak, people pattern their lives, knowingly or unknowingly, after the behavior of those they admire and respect. A person who holds respect for another can readily be motivated by that person. Respect and admiration must be earned as they are inherent through education, decisiveness, background, heritage, interest, fame or numerous other qualities. The tendency to follow one of respect need not be difficult, but it can be an elusive pursuit. Elusive because important relationships are continually changing, either being enhanced or deteriorating. Significant relationships cannot simply remain status quo. Frequently, individuals tend to have unrealistic expectations of those they wish to emulate. In such situations, respect is lost when the individual does not meet such expectations.

Respect would seem best capitalized on when viewed as a motivating force emanating from initial impact. Long-term respect is common, but impact, assisting one to move to action, diminishes with time. A manager, for instance, would set the tone for office standards, authority would command and carry through into implementation, but only respect can create the willingness to act. No one is respected for everything, and a person who has gained the respect of others has no control over the intensity of magnitude of the respect offered. Being accorded respect carries with it a strong sense of responsibility and the manner in which that responsibility is handled can permanently affect the lives of others.

Idol Image

When one idolizes another, he places that person above him with respect to such traits as status, intelligence, income and so forth. Admiring someone in and of itself is not unfavorable, as long as such individuals are not being placed in a God-like position.[27] Following in the footsteps of an idol image and patterning an action after another would most often be, as Emerson put it, "Suicide."[28] Imitation will usually only lead to a dead end. Each person has unique qualities to express and no one can express them in a like manner. Creativity is often stifled by copying or following the actions of others too closely. By taking the strong points and ignoring those aspects that do not fit into a comfortable or designed plan of action, one can benefit through direct, rather than, second-hand insight.

Trust

Trust can best be defined as a firm belief in the honesty, reliability and ability of another and confident expectation to commit something to another's care. Trust in someone is an earned trait. Admiration, respect and similar traits have not much to do with trust. Trust can be a real moving factor.

When someone places personal trust in another, it is as if he is saying, "Take over, I trust you to do the job as well or better than I can."

Trust is not necessarily quickly gained, but it can be lost in an instant. To re-establish trust is a difficult task, because building reliability takes time and focus. Trust gained places one in a select group — it should be honored.

Fear

Not uncommon are the myriad of threatening statements heard around an office, at home, or in most average daily activities. The basic intent of such statements is to evoke fear in someone. Using fear to resolve a problem has proved to be ineffective, primarily resulting in more problems.

"Jack will probably get the promotion because your work has not been adequate."

"We may have to move you out of this office if you don't start producing."

"If you don't get to work on time, we'll have to let you go."

Statements such as these merely serve to change certain behavior, and then for only short periods of time. They usually do not assist in releasing Vital Enthusiasm and, more often than not, enlarge the problem areas by using negative referral. Fear cannot be used as a threatening tool on a self-confident person — one who knows his job and his position in life. Beyond that, such individuals, generally, do not attract adverse opinions. Most

Outer Conditioning

likely a problem has existed for some time and, through poor management, the problem has gone unchecked. The fear-evoking statements are used by one who is inept in the skills of communication and human behavior.

Summary

The management of anything can be considered to be a professional enterprise. Unfortunately, however, many managers fall into the "crisis management" category, resulting in their decisions being poorly thought out and acting as though they had been inspired from the heavens above. The manager's constructive imagination is governed by an orderly mind viewing the possibilities, analyzing the difficulties, and controlling the execution of the decision(s). A manager must possess forethought to plot new paths and be able to assemble the necessary people to achieve action-oriented decisions.

Up to this point, we have dealt with the personal aspects of inner qualities and outer conditioning. Both are human qualities that could cause one to release Vital Enthusiasm. Specific methods of the release of Vital Enthusiasm for individual expression will be discussed and evaluated in subsequent chapters.

[24]Dr. Thomas Gordon, *Parent Effectiveness Training* (New York: Peter H. Wyden Inc., 1970), p. 115.

[25]A Collection of Monthly Letter, *Of Interest to Executives* (Montreal, Quebec: The Royal Bank of Canada, 1955), p. 65.

[26]Albert Einstein, *Ideas and Opinions* (New York: Dell Publishing Co., Inc., 1954), p. 65.

[27]Joseph S. Benner, *The Impersonal Life* (San Gabriel, California: C.A.Willing, 1973), p. 126.

[28]Ralph Waldo Emerson, *Emerson's Essays* (New York: Thomas Y. Crowell Co., 1926), p. 32.

IV

Results Phase

Results Phase

A. THOUGHT FORMULATION, a reliable tool for success and a logical preface to desire.

In physics it is called the law of impenetrability, i.e., "no two objects can occupy the same space at the same time." In the mental realm it works similarly — "no two thoughts can occupy the same mind at the same instant."

Thoughts of every nature are available to us at all times — success, failure, love, discontent. Thoughts of the office with a window overlooking the city and thoughts of the last run-in with the boss are ever present. Yes, thoughts can be selected, but one, and only one prime thought can occupy the mind at any moment in time.

Thoughts originate in various ways: (1) An individual's need-level determines many thoughts with the hierarchy or ranking of needs being the basis for evaluating one's present level of thinking. Thus, understanding the needs of an individual provides for better understanding of the nature of one's desires. (2) Because thoughts may occupy space in the mind through catalysts other than basic needs or desire, one may be influenced by his surroundings, visual and audio stimuli, causing fleeting thoughts to enter. Such thoughts may remain or depart rapidly — the length of their stay will basically depend upon two factors:

1. The degree of individual emotional involvement with others, with current situations, and so forth;

2. The level of mental discipline commanded by the individual.

Alarming noises or actions catch the attention of the listener. Bankruptcy, personal disaster and the like also catch one's attention, especially when personally involved. However, merely having one's attention does not provide for longevity or the need to meditate on the problem. Yet, this is generally how individuals react under such conditions. Often they tend to harbor such thoughts for far too long a time. Equally alarming thoughts may be released and replaced by others, so also can the negatively associated thoughts of bankruptcy and personal disaster be replaced. At such times disciplined and trained minds excel with the true value of focused thinking revealed. These are commonalities shared among great thinkers, coupled with the dedication and understanding needed to bring ideas into physical realities.

A third way thoughts originate must be acknowledged as not only a source of thought, but also as a source of desire, i.e., that being hunch, intuitive impression or insight. Call it what you will, everyone, at some time or another, has been blessed with guidance. Regardless of the form, intuitiveness occurs, without explanation, from some seemingly external force or impetus. An idea germinates from inside one's own being, seemingly having no association with the outside world. An idea or thought form that has not necessarily been included in one's past experience though, to some degree, may proceed out of it as an expansion of fuller expression of the idea. This is the thought form that fathered the idea this writer believes to be the inception of desire and becomes the spark that feeds Vital Enthusiasm.

Realizing the presence of intuitive thought forces one to acknowledge that it is both creative and directive. Intuitiveness determines the actual forms under which the conditions for its manifestation will take in one's own particular world, as well as supplying the energy for their production.[29]

With respect to the two previously mentioned areas which give rise to thought, i.e., need and environment, the third, the guidance system is probably the prime cause in forming one's outer world, both attitudinal and situational. The point has been missed by the reader if he cannot relate his thinking to the inception of desire.

If this thought-forming power is to be specifically directed toward personal achievement, one must learn to rely upon the impressions received. The question arises, "How effective are these impressions and can they be constructively applied to business?"

THOUGHT FORMULATION 53

Results Phase

The idea that successful company executives manage business activities by using intuitive impressions might seem farfetched. Yet, in a 10-year research project at Newark College of Engineering, it was found that the better executives, defined as the ones who make superior profits for their companies, rely more on intuitive impressions in making decisions for their companies than the less superior executives.[30]

After completing the research project, Douglas Dean, co-author, concluded that top executives have to be unusual people. Such individuals are forced to make decisions for their companies even when they do not have all the necessary facts. Dean said that such executives must cultivate the ability to tune into themselves for answers to questions for which there is no readily apparent physical data. The higher up the executive ladder a person progresses, the more the decision will deal with the unknown — and the less valid, less reliable and less available will be the data used to make corporate decisions. This means that in addition to having superior decision-making ability, top executives also have the need for an intuitive component in their decision-making ability. Executives are not judged for good decisions but, rather, they are judged on good outcomes.

Like any other talent, the intuitive aspect of the individual, which seems to be inherent within everyone, needs to be cultivated if it is to grow. Acknowledgement that it exists will be the point of beginning — from there, usage is important.

Many top executives have publicly acknowledged their use of intuition as a tool in decision-making functions. William W. Keeler, retired board chairman of Phillips Petroleum, attributed much of his business success to strong intuitive feelings of which he had been aware for at least 30 years. When Keeler talked about strong gut feelings, he pointed to the solar plexus (stomach) stating, "I get to feeling it right here, and it is very strong. In fact, it sometimes is so strong I think of it as a fact." John L. Tishman, former executive officer of Tishman Realty & Construction Co., candidly acknowledged the importance of intuition in business decision-making. He said that few decisions are arrived at in a wholly objective manner. Somewhere along the line, subjectivity creeps into the decision-making process: "Everything, no matter how it appears wrapped in facts and figures, is ultimately reliant upon some assumptions that somebody has made intuitively, perhaps three or four times removed from the top executive."

Alexander M. Poniatoff, founder of Ampex Corporation, said that, "When the unconscious mind knows the answer, it then tries to influence or interfere with the conscious mind's logical conclusions. I think this is intuition." John E. Fetzer, then chairman of the board of Fetzer Broadcasting Company, said he picked management people for his business enterprises largely through intuition. "I literally order the subconscious mind to do research and come up with answers. The unknowns of yesterday are accepted scientific facts of today, and this will be repeated ad infinitum." Eleanor Fried, the businesswoman who was responsible for spearheading the best-selling book, *Jonathan Livingston Seagull*, stated, "In deciding whether I want to handle a project or whether something that's brought to me will be successful, I depend on my feeling side, my intuition." Sydney S. Baron served as a management consultant to businesses which collectively represented sales of about $60 billion yearly. In dealing with these pragmatic, successful enterprises, Baron remarked that his counsel is based 80 percent on intuition, 10 percent on logic, and 10 percent on experience. He also said that all of the successful people he had associated with relied heavily on intuition for decision-making. When chatting with potential clients, Baron revealed that he knew within the first 60 seconds whether potential clients would retain him.

Louis H. Golden, then president of Commodity Steel & Processing, Inc., Madison Heights, Mich., stated that when recognized and listened to, precognition and use of intuition had led to important success during his business career. "My intuitive feelings are like an inner impression, throwing light on a problem in a secure and reassuring way." Golden also said, "A person will get impressions or ideas or gut feelings, but doesn't always listen to them. In the past, I've been hurt because I didn't pay attention to these feelings." Patrick Price, then chief executive officer for Princess Coal Company in Huntington, West Virginia, referred to himself as, "One who operates with or without a body." Price was not playing word games. Scientific research has shown that one can "exteriorize" his conscious self to obtain data and information through intuition. "By virtue of the fact that I have come forward to state this," said Price, "it can help unlock doors for those in business . . . they can either challenge what I say and do, or they can accept it and apply it to self."[31]

These are just a few of the many successful people who have publicly stated their acknowledgement of, and reliance on, the intuitive process. To put it another way, "a vague feeling, perhaps of discomfort, a flash, an idea, too often diagnosed by logic as indigestion or fantasy." Small wonder any of us hear the intuitive voice which has added to the invention of the light bulb, television and atomic energy. Successful listening is the key to our minds.

To briefly summarize, then, the first step of the results phase, i.e., Thought Formation and the inception of desire, suggests that individuals acknowledge:

1. Attention getters — alarming the senses, sounds, sights, and so forth.
2. Environmental and need levels.
3. Intuition.

B. IMAGERY vs. CREATIVE IMAGINATION

The process of mental imagery is probably the most widely acknowledged, yet least effectively applied, mental tool of the human race. Imagery is based on one thing — thinking; and every living human thinks. Often, people say that they cannot visualize, but in reality they have simply not cultivated their basic mental picturing capabilities. In order to do so, individuals must remember that the basis for all mental visualization involves the thinking process.

Results Phase

Imagery is a natural process. It is not forced, it is the by-product of one's thought processes. In visualizing, or making a mental picture, one is not endeavoring to change the laws of nature; instead, one is attempting to fulfill them.[32]

Imagery and creative imagination are usually discussed as one. But the real difference between mental imagery and creative imagination is that mental imagery is the image formed in the mind when the thought occurs. Creative imagination, on the other hand, is how one develops this image for constructive purposes and incorporates it into his life plan or goal.

A few of the benefits of mental imagery were discussed in the section on self-esteem. However, to gain the understanding necessary for practical implementation into one's business or personal life, a slightly more detailed analysis is offered here.

Feelings developed utilizing mental imagery tend to influence our actions and behavior.

When one thinks of the word "circus," it conjures up various mental pictures, e.g., animals, clowns, music, jugglers, trapeze artists, and so forth. But not many people would stop with just the written word of CIRCUS. It is natural to think in pictures. It is natural to create mental images in the mind.

Sitting idly, passively and merely forming mental pictures is not an intelligent use of the inherent visionary process. Rather, one should strive to gain an element of control, thereby allowing a predetermined end to ensue. Al Pollard, management consultant and businessman of Little Rock, Ark., told how he introduced the intuitive nature within each of us to the business community. He called it "picturizing." He proposed that if you concentrate on something you want and picturize it in your mind — without fail — it will somehow eventually materialize for you.

> "It's a system of creative thinking we can work at every day, not permitting fears or worries or setbacks or disappointments to upset our pictures. These pictures become the blueprints our creative power of mind uses to magnetize and attract to us conditions, circumstances, opportunities, resources, and even the people to help materialize for us in the real life what we have visualized — be it good or bad. Now I've also found that everyone of us has the capability of visualizing the projects we desire to become reality. It seems to me the energy of thought is transmitted into matter."[33]

When people's eyes are open, images emanate from external sources — sources outside their own bodies and psyche. People see other people, buildings, automobiles, animals and the like, and generally take for granted that such objects are separate from them. Also, as people's eyes are closed, similar mental images come to mind. Such thoughts appear to be within one's own mind. Additionally, past events, memories of loved ones, familiar places and, often, daydreams of coming events, some far into the future, are seen the same way. Many people accredit little importance to these mental images, brushing them off as being unreal. The real experience, they say, is in the external world and the mental images that are developed are unreal and

Results Phase

have no significant value with regard to their daily lives.

Similarly, many people feel they do not understand the workings of their mental picturing device abilities but are quite well-versed regarding outer world events. Most people are convinced of the separateness of the two worlds. Yet, studies indicate that an individual cannot tell the difference between something seen physically and one vividly imagined and in great detail.[34]

Imagery as Related to Physical Impressions

"What you see is what you get!" is a common statement which has universal understanding. Dr. Frederick J. Eikerenkoetter II, better known as "Reverend Ike," said that, "What you see is what you become." At first, this may seem to be a bold statement, but further research has suggested that one tends to respond in a very physical way to the images placed in the mind — real or unreal.

Even in the physical world, i.e., using physical images as viewed through the eyes, one frequently responds in a manner which would be uncalled for if the total image were revealed. An example is the story of six blind men each standing near a different part of an elephant and describing their individual interpretations of the object before them; each describes something different. The same problem can arise for one who is sighted. When driving in traffic, great difficulty can occur when attempting to predict conditions ahead. On occasion, one may judge incorrectly, e.g., his decision to change lanes, to pass

Results Phase

another automobile, or even whether to travel, is
often decided by how the traffic appears to be at the
moment. Subsequently, one tends to use as the basis
for such decisions, the results of the images perceived. A helicopter passing overhead will use the
total overview to derive such decisions.

Another example is that of someone sitting on
a park bench, enjoying the music from a portable
radio. A news flash breaks into the music and reports
that a giant gorilla has escaped from the zoo. The
music returns and shortly thereafter the individual
feels a tapping on his shoulder. Upon turning around,
he discovers that it is the giant gorilla doing the
tapping. The individual has only two options — flee
or stand and fight. Our friend decides to flee, leaping
to his feet and frantically running through the park
with his heart going faster than his feet. Suddenly,
someone behind him is laughing hysterically —
Guess who? — It is a friend dressed in a gorilla
costume. Did he respond? Yes! Was it real? No! In the
physical world, when the whole picture is not seen,
an avoidance of a particular reaction is usually not
possible.

When viewing television or a movie, one sits
comfortably observing the still images rapidly being
flashed on the screen, giving the appearance of
movement. Feelings are created, tears may form,
sounds of laughter may be heard and the response by
individuals to a physically created still image
becomes obvious.

Court testimonies are often based on what an
individual has seen. But the eye's accuracy is often
questioned due to such variables as darkness,

weather conditions, physical similarities in appearance or dress. Emotional unreliability generally occurs when one sees blood or other such situations that are not regularly encountered. Under such conditions, the individual's tendency is to retreat, to faint, and thereby focus on something other than the actual event. One does respond to what is seen in the physical world and, often, it does produce an actual physical response.

Imagery as Related to Mental Impressions

FORMING MENTAL IMAGE — FOCUS — PHYSICAL REALITY

⟶ Progressive Intensity ⟶

(Figure 2)

Just as with physical images, mental images cause a physiological response. In the physical world, one might sit in a theater watching a movie, and if the movie is not entertaining or is disturbing in some way, he may leave. It would be fruitless for anyone who is not pleased with the film they are viewing to attempt to beat up the screen in the hope that the film would improve. In the physical world, such is not possible. A better solution would be to change the film in the motion picture projector, thus providing a new image on the screen.

Mental images work in a similar fashion. Reactions to them are in the physical world. The strange thing is that images continue to flash on the screen of the mind which are not conducive to the life-style one desires to live. Often, attempts are made to beat up the screen (blaming outer circumstances), for bad experiences in one's life. Mental pictures tend to flash in the mind which produced undesired feelings and situations. Such negatives are primarily due to our own mental projector. To enhance a particularly positive experience, one must first envision it as being accomplished in the mind through proper thought formulation. It has been said time and time again: "Nothing is either good or bad, but thinking makes it so." There is neither a good nor bad situation; it is the attitude that one has toward it that makes it what it is. As thought processes occur, each individual tends to react to such thoughts.[35]

Personal opinions may enter into the results process by influencing one to react in a particularly negative manner. When an image or thought crosses the mind, most people are anxious or fearful that others may not respond positively. One must be certain that such negativeness has not been created from within and ensure that the whole picture has been viewed. Often thoughts of low self-esteem produce narrowness of scope, thus drastically inhibiting the desired manifestation of situations.

When individuals sense a lack of respect, they are uncomfortable in the presence of certain other employees or their employer. This may cause tension and interactions that will actually produce the very thing feared. This situation generally stems from childhood. Habits are developed, habits in thinking that dictate the belief, "they like me for what I do, not for what I am." When one mistakes performance approval with personal approval, there is a good chance that some work is needed in distinguishing between the two. If this pattern of thinking goes uncorrected, adulthood will be reached with a warped concept of individual worth. Lack of understanding and low self-esteem can contribute to failure in any endeavor.[36]

More often than not, people-pleasing images tend to create demeaning reactions. Again, such images are developed from childhood, partly because of being told to pay attention to parents' wishes, by pleasing them with good grades, degrees, promotions, job titles, and otherwise keeping up with the Joneses! With such an attitude the need to "show" others and "please" others becomes part of a lifestyle.[37]

Mental imagery as applied to role playing is also an effective tool in business — for instance, when seeking a job. William Marston, a psychologist who developed a system of visualization called "rehearsal practice," tells how to improve confidence during a job interview. He suggests that one plan in advance and go over possible questions, thereby rehearsing the interview. Marston says that even if none of the rehearsed questions are asked, the rehearsal practice is still valuable because it builds confidence and helps a person ad-lib and be spontaneous. Marston goes on to say that people always act out a role in life, so they may as well choose a successful role, and keep rehearsing it.[38]

Role-playing is in keeping with the initial perspective of mental imagery affecting physical response. When someone is extremely cold, thinking warm can take away such discomfort. What happens? Skin temperature increases and warmth is experienced. Now it is not true to say one is warm when one is actually cold, but in truth, thinking warmth generates an increase in body temperature. It is important to realize that such concepts can bring desired results into one's life.[39]

Creative imagination can be used from the most simple of daily situations to the very complex. An averge situation in which both negative and positive, as well as creative thought patterns of imagery can be seen in this example: An employee is seeking a raise in pay, having worked at the job for several years and feeling deserving in every way for the good work, punctuality, and responsibility that has been displayed.

When imagining the sequence of events that will take place, the employee in our example pictures

Results Phase

a timid, subservient approach because he doesn't want to disturb the boss's privacy. He harbors a feeling of, "he's too busy to see me," but he makes the approach. Nervousness and fidgeting stem from imagination and the thought occurs to our friend whether the raise is really needed at this time. The feeling is to delay it until next week, next month or next year. Worry about phrasing the question properly, what he'll think and the firmness of delivery, are all concerns in the mind of our friend. When the failure approach is taken, failure is often the result.

With creative imagination, again a mental picture is formed, but this time a confident knock on the door is pictured, body posture and gestures are confident because of a deserving feeling. The imagined interaction takes place with sureness and a feeling of respect of a job well done, and both parties acknowledge this. Certainly one would be in a better position of receiving a raise with this attitude.

If we picture ourselves functioning in specific situations, it is nearly the same as the actual performance. Mental practice helps to perform better in real life.[40]

Like everything else, role-playing and creative imagination take practice. Taking time to devote sincere interest in mental picturing, paying attention to every detail and involving as many mental senses as possible are beneficial. In the innermost part of the mind, sense what the situation would actually be like if the desired result were unfolding this very moment. Incorporate the senses of touch, smell, sight, sound, and yes, even taste, into the mental picture. Feel the emotion of the moment, as though it is an actuality. Like an actor, run through this in the actual time frame, if possible.

Applications to business and personal life are too numerous to mention here. The reader is asked to carry this further into his or her personal life to describe in detail areas that have previously been uncomfortable. Personal interactions, business presentations, children confrontations, testing situations, physical abilities, all these and more can be enhanced through the imagery process.

Imagery as Applied to Health

Imagery in health needs special attention because there are so many people in our society who are continually plagued with physical disabilities due to stress. Success, as it is termed in this writing, depends largely on one's health. An extensive study will not be undertaken here, but here are some points on how to overcome many day-to-day health problems.

Executive stress is probably one of the most common diseases in today's corporate world. Business people hurry, push, overdo, all for the proverbial deadline. One factor that is not normally considered is that it is not possible to catch stress as one catches a cold; it must be created. Stress, although usually considered negative, does not have to be so. Various types of life experiences will create both pleasant and unpleasant stress.[41]

Mental tensions, frustrations, insecurity and aimlessness are among the most damaging stressors, and psychosomatic studies have shown how often they cause migraine headaches, peptic ulcers, heart attacks, hypertension, mental disease, suicide, or just hopeless unhappiness.

No one likes to become ill, and yet maintaining the natural state of health takes time and dedication, especially in today's world of fast foods, chemical stimulants and rapidly paced life-styles. The body is continually changing, and if one is to maintain or improve the physical condition, a maintenance plan is mandatory.

Intuition relays many messages to the individual, but often people don't listen. Feelings of anxiety, shortness of breath, worry, depression, pain in any form, are all messages. Many go to work when they don't feel well because sick leave has been used up or the job must get done. Statements like, "That's a big boy," or "That's my man," encourage them to keep going when the body is sending opposing messages. Ralph Waldo Emerson stated, "First be a good animal," and the truth in that statement is one that would be well taken by many of today's business people.

When animals become ill, they generally retire to a quiet place to sleep. Intuition (or insight) is a dominant factor in an animal's make-up. Through insight into the simplicity of life, one can learn lessons that can be directly applied at the human level.[42]

Health Considerations and Suggestions

A variety of suggestions is offered to the reader to show the versatility and effectiveness of mental imagery and attitude related to an individual's physical and mental health.

Laughter Therapy

If negative emotions produce negative chemical changes in the body, wouldn't positive emotions produce positive chemical changes? Is it possible that love, hope, faith, laughter, confidence and the will to live have therapeutic value? Do chemical changes occur only on the downside?[43] Norman Cousins posed these questions after he was given one chance in 500 to live. Admittedly, this is an isolated case, however the value of such dramatic results must, at least, be acknowledged.

In brief, Cousins was suffering from a serious collagen illness and was not given much hope. It was at that point he thought it would be good to actively participate in his recovery rather than just be a passive observer. Although not an M.D. himself, Cousins became knowledgeable about his own disease. With large does of ascorbic acid (vitamin C), *and large doses of laughter* he began the recovery process. He discovered that 10 minutes of genuine belly laughter had an anesthetic effect and would allow him two hours of pain-free sleep. His discovery led him to never underestimate the capacity of the human mind and body to regenerate.[44]

Developing a Youthful Attitude

Maintaining a youthful outlook will allow the flexibility necessary for the constant changes and decisions an executive must make.[45] Along with laughter, smiling should be cultivated since it lifts the face and creates a sparkle in the eyes.

The aging process has much to do with the state of mind. Through worry, stress, and undue concern for matters in one's life, the aging process is accelerated. Tell-tale signs of aging are everywhere. Notice the way an individual walks; there is such a thing as a youthful walk, a fat walk, an old walk. By imagining oneself as youthful, it seems that the body responds to this and springs into action to comply with the vision imagined.

Energy flows in, through and around every individual at all times. Such energy is a natural phenomenon of life. Why, then, do some express this force so vibrantly while others exhibit no visible signs of vitality? The answer is simple: it has to do with imagining. Even in youth, one can fall prey to a lack of enthusiasm. Picture a young boy mowing the lawn on a warm summer day: sometimes it may look as though the lawn mower is holding the youngster up — no enthusaism! No zest! Along comes the chance for a baseball game and the boy leaves . . . what happened? Where did the energy come from? It was always there; all that was needed was to change the picture in the mind and the body responded in like manner.

Put cheerfulness in the voice, spark in the walk, and a youthful appearance will naturally follow. Change to the young is generally non-resistant. Change to the old is less easily accomplished. One noted American psychologist said, "To effect change becomes increasingly difficult, and requires purposeful effort to counteract a system already established."[46] Most people interpret that to mean: "You can't teach an old dog new tricks." No habit, whether new or long-established, can grip and hold anyone by its intrinsic strength. Habits have no strength of their own.[47] Just as it is necessary to change old, inhibiting, mental thought patterns to allow for new creative imagination input, so it is also necessary to change physically to remain youthful.

Degrees of flexibility or rigidity can be measured on the index of flexibility. Resistance to change often is marked by old thinking habits, whereas a more flexible attitude and open mind can help express much of the youth that life has to offer. Either extreme is not beneficial, since there are those who enjoy novelty and change, while others can be relied upon to oppose a new idea with vigor. People near the opposite ends of the flexibility index can be labeled "creatures of habit" and "creatures of novelty."

It has been found that the more knowledgeable a person is regarding an issue, the more likely he is to review his first reaction critically. If he lacks knowledge, he will probably not modify his first response. Thus rigidity or flexibility tendencies reflect proportionately the amount of knowledge the receiver possesses.[48]

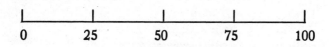

0	25	50	75	100

Figure: 3 Index of Flexibility

Results Phase

Beliefs in Aging

In a study on aging conducted in South Africa, children of three tribes were asked how long their mothers and fathers live. The answers ranged between 120 and 130. Then the parents in the tribes were asked about their life expectancy and the answer was much the same. The average age in these cultures is 120 to 130 years.[49]

What is the average length of life in America? Seventy years is a common answer, but certainly not 120 years. What is the reason for the difference? With the technological advancements in this country, one would think that life expectancy would be longer than in most cultures. Belief seems to play an important role in reaching the later years — a belief that it is normal to do this, that it is normal to live to an unbelievable ripe old age. Certainly other factors are involved, but beliefs do greatly influence the outcome. Regarding cures of organic diseases, Sir William Osler believed the cure was not brought essentially by the treatment used, but by the patient's faith in the effectiveness of the treatment and the comfort provided by good nursing care.[50] Studies show that up to 90 percent of patients who reach out for medical help are suffering from self-limiting disorders well within the range of the body's own healing powers.[51]

The Value of Health Maintenance vs. Surgery and Other Physical Aids

Although mental imagery has proved to be effective in health maintenance and even in the reversing of a given disease, at times physical assistance is needed and even recommended.

If a particular problem exists within an individual's body and an aggressive plan of mental healing has been implemented with limited or no results, the situation must be handled in some other manner. An urgent situation demands action in some form or another and the body's need for attention is the prime factor. An acute problem, such as an auto accident, heart attack and the like, needs immediate attention either mentally or physically. Suffice to say that if the mental attitude of the individual were, prior to the incident, focused on health, calmness, and thoughts in tune with life, medical assistance may not have been required. It is possible that, even at an acute stage, with proper action of thought, mental and physical illness could be turned into positive results and development.

Most likely, however, a physical aid of some sort would be useful to place the body into a state, through medicine or surgery, in which the healing process could be believable to the injured individual. Before submitting to surgery, when possible, the patient should have received answers to such questions as:

1. Why is this operation necessary?
2. What are the risks and complications?
3. What are the risks without surgery?
4. Are there alternative courses of treatment which don't involve surgery and what are the corresponding chances of recovery?

Surgery can never be undone, and the risks should be known and evaluated by all who decide to undergo this process. It has been found that while a surgeon may cite a 75 percent success rate, the remaining 25 percent of failures sometimes result in worse conditions after surgery and produce long-lasting problems that didn't exist before.[52] Surgery is not being discouraged here, rather, patients are merely advised to weigh the risks. Each person must treat the situation as an individual; statistics can never accurately reflect a specific situation. Where possible, several opinions about the necessity of the surgery should be sought. A rushed attitude to "get it over with" is, more often that not, regretted. It does appear that all such treatment is aimed at the patient as a body, not at the patient as a person.

Illness as a Catalyst for Change

An individual draws experiences in order to learn. This is not necessarily a conscious decision, but one nonetheless that exists through subconscious impressions, guilts, beliefs, self-defeating behaviors and the like. One does not draw an experience into existence that he cannot cope with. Recognizing this may cause some to probe deeper into one's illness, root out the lesson, and thus, in many cases, resolve the problem.

Simple acknowledgement that one must change a life-style through attitude and behavior adjustment is a motivating force toward change for some people. When the body is demanding attention through pain (one of the strongest voices it can use), it often causes an individual to redirect in such ways as overridding the social conditions, adapting assertive behavior, attention to self; an infinite variety of needs may be heeded. It is essential to recognize that the needs being met through the illness are fully legitimate and deserve to be met. From this viewpoint, the intent of the bodily message is constructive, even in illness. Illness can be an opportunity for an individual to achieve emotional growth.[53]

Affecting the Physiological State with Mental Imagery

The placebo effect is well known to be a method used to allow the body to heal itself by itself. Although a physical aid, the influence of the mind on the body is significant. The placebo effect is used in medicine today, by itself and in conjunction with other drugs, allowing the mind of the individual to exercise its own healing abilities on the body.[54]

Bio-Feedback

Research in bio-feedback is advancing rapidly. Basic studies have discovered that any person wishing to exercise control over the body's involuntary control system may do so by incorporating the process of bio-feedback.[55] Bio-feedback is simply monitoring the bodily conditions and feeding them back so that they can be charted. A most simple form of this is taking one's own pulse. The individual grasps his wrists and notices the pulse beating. This is bio-feedback.

Electronic devices have made this process much more accurate and reliable. With the use of these monitoring devices, one can observe the heart beat, blood pressure, body temperature, and numerous other functions. In addition to monitoring these functions, a high degree of conscious bodily control may be achieved.

Psychosomatic Health

The term psychosomatic disease is often heard, however, few people are acquainted with the reverse, psychosomatic health. General consensus holds that psychosomatic disease is not real, that it simply exists as "all in the head." While it is true that the psychological make-up of the individual is the major contributing factor to a psychosomatic disease, it is, nonetheless, a real experience to the physical body. An ulcer may have developed through an anxious or tense state of mind; this does not make the ulcer any less real. A simple headache from tension or over-work expresses itself as very real to the individual, just as though it was acquired through a form of physical abuse. Almost everyone acknowledges the psychosomatic connection in high blood pressure, heart attacks and headaches. It is this author's opinion that this psychosomatic effect touches not only these areas, but also is a major factor in the acquisition and recovery of every human malady, however severe. Dr. Eugene P. Pendergrass, president of the American Cancer Society, emphasized the necessity of treating the whole patient, not just the physical body. He states: "Within one's mind is a power capable of exerting forces which can either enhance or inhibit the progress of a disease."[56]

In a two-year study conducted by Dr. O. Carl

Simonton on cancer, 152 patients were treated. The attitudes in Figure 4 show their willingness to take part in and consciously exercise their mental visualization abilities toward a positive result with their particular disease.[57]

PATIENT ATTITUDE						
		Uncooperative — doesn't follow instructions.	Uncooperative — rarely follows instructions.	Usually follows instructions	Follows instructions and shows some initiative	Full cooperation, follows instructions. implicitly & is enthusiastic about getting better.	
		– –	–	+ –	+	+ +	
PATIENT RESPONSE	Marked relief of symptoms & dynamic improvement of condition — Excellent	0	0	0	11	9	20
	Relief of symtoms, general condition improved — Good	0	2	34	31	0	67
	Mild relief of symptoms — Fair	0	14	29	0	0	43
	No relief of symptoms — Poor	2	17	3	0	0	22
	Totals	2	33	66	42	9	152

(Figure 4)

Results Phase

Simonton found that patients who "follow instructions implicitly and are enthusiastic about getting better, show marked relief of symptoms and dramatic improvement of their condition (nine out of nine patients)." The implications of a study such as Simonton's are that a person's visualizations play a fundamental role in the cause of disease and its cure.

Considering the studies on stress, biofeedback, placebos, patient attitude related to recovery response, and numerous other factors, it appears that attitude and mental imagery techniques have a profound influence on the direction a bodily disease will take. Dr. Elmer Green of the Menninger Foundation states: "Every change in the physiological state is accompanied by an appropriate change in the mental and emotional state, conscious or unconscious, and conversely, every change in the mental and emotional state, conscious or unconscious, is accompanied by an appropriate change in the physiological state."[58] One is led to conclude that the mind can relieve illnesses as well as create them.

Technique of Mental Imagery
Visualization or Picturing

In concluding this segment on health maintenance, one final area must be covered, that being the technique of mental imagery. Many variations of this visualization process have been offered by other authors and the process that is about to be described is intended to act as a guideline. It is basic in its description, but can be adapted to fit the needs and desires of an individual.

Results Phase

Because mental imagery is a natural process, the discussion here centers on the effective use of this process for greater results orientation. Although it is known that any thought will cause a physiological effect, the major purpose of visualization is to direct the thinking process toward a speedy end result. It is most favorable if this can be accomplished at will.

One often tends to allow negative fears and anxieties to occupy the mind, forming pictures of an unwanted result. These pictures are extremely powerful with emotional involvement and strong feeling tied to them. Forming vivid mental pictures at will, while mustering up the strength of emotional power with direct focus toward a specific desire, can be accomplished through the following exercise:

Sit or lie in a comfortable position. The arms and legs should be uncrossed to allow freedom of circulation throughout the body. Tight clothing should be loosened and any other garment or piece of equipment that might be distracting, such as hearing aid or eyeglasses, should be removed. Why sit or lie? Why not stand or walk? Mental picturing can be and is done at all times. Sitting or lying is generally more conducive to a concentrated effort. The sitting position lends itself to a more logical train of thought, while lying tends to be associated with a more receptive, relaxing state. Try to think about a solution to a problem while lying flat on the back, then think about the same thing while sitting upright. Notice that maintaining a directed, logical stream of thought is much easier in the upright position. This can be understood as a function of two different organismic states, indicated by postural changes alone. It is possible to think logically while supine, but it is more difficult.[59]

Although many recommend that mental imaging be done with the eyes closed, it is not the "only way." There are advantages to closed eyes, such as assisting the relaxation process and eliminating visual stimulation. Mental picturing, however, can be accomplished eyes open or closed in either state.[60] One aspect that is helpful to affect bodily changes is triggering the alpha state of mind, a brain impulse of 7 to 14 cycles per second. Most people seem to be able to acquire this slowing down of brain wave pattern, from beta wave — 14cps and above — by becoming relaxed and closing their eyes.[61]

Rhythmic breathing will assist the relaxation process. Rhythmic breathing is known to relax the mind and body, as well as act as a cleanser for the body. A few deep breaths to begin the process is helpful, lifting the shoulders high to allow the air to fill the upper portion of the lungs. This is not often done since it seems that most people are very much middle breathers, neither filling the upper portion of the lungs, nor the lower portion of the lungs. Shallow breathing is not healthy, and if one is to accentuate the picturing power, a finely tuned body is beneficial.[62]

In beginning the mental imagery process, the images seen in the eye are generally different from the images seen with the aid of the retina. As a rule, images resemble thoughts and ideas, rather than sights. Many people feel as though they are "making up" the images, rather than seeing them. This is a normal feeling for one beginning to experiment with this process.[63]

By allowing an image to form in the mind, and being non-judgmental as to whether it is clear, good or bad, would be a good way toward developing self-confidence in imaging. Practice makes perfect, and the more the mind is trained toward one particular focused desire, the easier and more familiar the method becomes. Two brief exercises are supplied here. The reader will note that these deal particularly with relationships. For the purpose of this writing, it was thought that this would be more appropriate and time-efficient. If one wishes to progress through a natural order of visualization exercises, from black and white stationary objects, to three-dimensional, moving colored objects involving the five senses, refer to the Samuels, Howard and Maltz research.[64]

Relationship Enhancing Visualization Exercises

This exercise can be used by an individual who realizes that tension exists on the job, possibly between employee and employer. Imagine a subject standing or sitting in a calm relaxed manner. Mentally look into the face of this person and particularly notice the eyes. What color are they? Imagine looking directly into this person's eyes with a confident and understanding poise. Notice the other features of the face, the nose and lips. The hair color and hairline can be observed also. Where is the hair parted? Is it curled or straight? How long is it? As the face is observed, notice that a relaxed feeling begins to be expressed and a feeling of responsiveness and receptivity is being created. Look at the rest of the person's body, noticing the person's clothing and how it is positioned. If the mental picture denotes a position similar to the usual resistant stance, mentally adjust the position for acceptance and openness. Now, mentally begin to converse with this person. Be especially concerned with the content of the conversation, making sure that all that is said is of a positive, caring and understanding nature. Listen to the tone of the other person's voice, soften it with your mental ear. Note the inflection, the volume. Finally, watch the person as the conversation ends. Mentally design an ending and parting to be of a cordial nature, one with an expectancy of picking up again where it left off.

This exercise could be considered to be a daydream about another person. If people realize that their daydreams are visualizations, they can use them as exercises for improving their image control.

The next exercise deals with self-visualizations. Many people have difficulty in creating a mental picture of themselves, so it may be helpful to use the mirror, watch home movies or look at pictures to make the mental imaging process easier. It is important that a clear mental picture of oneself is formed, especially when setting goals. Placing oneself "in" the mental picture makes a positive statement in the mind, and the mind must respond by doing its part for results orientation.

Self-confidence Visualization

Again follow the relaxation procedures with

the eyes closed. Following much the same pattern as above, mentally look directly straightforward, as in a mirror, absorbing the facial features, i.e., eyes, nose, ears, mouth, etc. To become comfortable with the mental image, it is good to create an animated face along with a totally animated figure. Observe the way the body is held and the way it moves. Mentally picture an activity that is done frequently, such as answering the telephone, typing or walking down the street.

Once the individual is comfortable and confident that he is seeing himself in the mental picture, he can move on to begin developing the aspect of self-confidence. Develop a mental mirror that reflects you, the person, as one possessing admirable traits — a likeable character, a person with confidence, decisiveness and receptivity to change. This is certainly an individual endeavor and the author can only speculate as to the feelings one should use to enhance the self-confidence. Rest assured, though, feelings must be incorporated into this mental picture to be successful in accomplishing a higher confidence level.

To recapture a feeling of confidence, it is helpful to recreate situations of a positive nature that have been experienced before. While capturing these "best moments," notice the feelings that were experienced. Take time to expand on this scene, seeing and feeling every detail in the imagination. Then, switch the picture to one of a desired situation and hold those same feelings of confidence. Incorporating all five senses into the scene is important to develop the situation into a real event in the mind.

Time taken on a daily basis will bring results

in visualization enhancement, as well as in the actual image projected. Do not become a slave to this routine: an hour a day in total is all that is suggested as a guideline.[65]

To capsulize the Imagery Vs. Creative Imagination section, the process described merely encourages the benefits to be derived. Through the related studies, observations and personal experience of the author, the belief exists that redirection of a given situation toward a desired result is possible. In business, management's role in visualization is critical, mainly because of the chain of communications and worker interactions encountered on a daily basis. Maintaining harmony and productivity is a great challenge for any manager. Decisiveness in management is important if harmony and productivity are to be gained. Careful deliberation of the alternatives of any decision requires analysis of the sequence in which alternative courses of action are present, identification of the range of alternatives at each stage, and comparative evaluation in order to make the right decision. It is possible to construct something like a decision tree, representing all the alternatives in their proper sequence.[66] This is rarely done in real life, and if one were to incorporate this list of ideas into the role-playing, mental picturing technique, it would greatly enhance the decision-making process.

The reader is asked to carry these ideas further into other business applications as well as to incorporate them into their personal lives, challenging the ideas by experimentation.

C. Spaced Repetition for Idea Embodiment

Every business should be eager to hire a trained, positive and enthusiastic employee, but how does one go about incorporating these qualities in employees who are presently on the job? The third step in the Results Phase relays a basic principle that, if employed, will ensure attentiveness to company goals and influence employees to move toward the desired result.

The practice of spaced repetition is commonly used by advertising firms to keep their product foremost in the public mind. It is used effectively on radio and television, in newspapers, magazines and organizational literature. The applications are virtually inexhaustable. Spaced repetition is a simple concept and works on the premise that whenever an idea is impressed consciously, over and over again, it creates a remembered thought pattern, and develops a feeling within the individual. This is the way actors learn their lines, singers learn songs, musicians play their instruments, etc. The reverse of spaced repetition is also one of the reasons for employee dissatisfaction, for the opposite end of this is sometimes recognized as inconsistency in management.

Spaced repetition is a natural by-product of individual thought and, as such, has had its introduction in the first two steps of the Results Phase already discussed:

1. Thought Formulation
   Basic premise: One's mind is capable of holding only one pure thought at a time.

Results Phase

2. Imagery vs. Creative Imagination
Basic premise: Pictures are always naturally created in the mind when one thinks.

Spaced repetition impacts the mind through constant bombardment of an idea. Thus, feeling is created. Although the mind remembers all, this quality is not often consciously exercised. Most people allow their memories to deteriorate to a point where they become very dependent upon lists for shopping and other tasks, reference books and other commonly used information sources. The author has no major quarrel with this, but to what length is this to be taken? Will the use of calculators become so commonplace that time will not be taken to memorize the multiplication tables?

In reality, everyone has a perfect memory: it is just a matter of recall. Perfect memory is known to exist because of various factors such as:

1. Electrostimulation of the brain. Because the brain has no feeling in this process, an electric needle may be placed on specific memory cells without causing irritation, directing a slight electrical charge through the cell, which causes a past memory to surface in a manner that is more than just a thought. It is recreated in the mind with feelings and emotions that were prominent at the time of the event. One may also be able to pay specific attention to details during this process, since all seem to be able to be recalled.

2. Emotional experiences. When asked to recall an experience from childhood, the tendency is to recall an emotional experience. There may be two reasons for this: emotional memory, which will be

the major subject in this portion, and eidetic memory. Eidetic memory is the remarkable phenomenon of a photographic memory possessed by many children. When trying to recall an historical fact, or the spelling of a word, they create a mental picture of the appropriate page in a textbook, and then they simply read off what they need to know. This valuable power rarely survives puberty. Perhaps the indiscriminate eidetic memory of childhood explains why the rememberances of early years are often so full of detail.[67]

Long-term emotional-type memories firmly establish themselves in the brain's complex file of thoughts and sensations, and most are capable of surviving electric shock, drugs, and sometimes even amnesia. The duration of a memory is partly determined by the importance of the material being remembered. Since the events remembered best and longest are those with the highest emotional charge, some scientists think the brain's emotional centers help determine which memories are short and which are long.[68] Most people above a certain age will remember when John F. Kennedy was assassinated, as well as where they were and the public events at the moment. Some events burn themselves into the memory simply and purely because of the intensity of the emotional charge that accompanies them.

3. Hypnosis. It may be difficult to remember the meal at lunch last Wednesday, however, in a state of hypnosis, last Wednesday's lunch, and last year's as well, could be readily remembered. Furthermore, such recall would include luncheon companions, the quality of the food, and what kind of day it was. This

is just another example of one's mental capability. The mind tends not to forget, rather, it is more a matter of recall.

The hypnotic state is defined as a "heightened ability of the subject to receive and follow instituted suggestions."[69] Hypnosis is not recommended as a method for memory recall, rather, it is presented here for the point of clarification. Hypnosis is a word often misunderstood, and it is sometimes connected with the occult. Actually, hypnotism is a normal phenomenon, and the power to hypnotize or to be hypnotized is latent in every individual. Essentially, all hypnosis is self-hypnosis.[70] The more deeply absorbed in an activity, the greater the tendency to experience a hypnotic state. Self-hypnosis can result when one becomes absorbed in reading a book, in work, in viewing a motion picture or a TV program, while listening to an interesting talk, and even during some religious ceremonies. Any strong emotion may also produce a state of hypnosis. The realization that states of self-hypnosis are common in such circumstances may provide a better understanding of it.

Psychologist David McClelland of Harvard says that people talk to themselves all the time in a state he calls "reverie." McClelland says that's all right, but the problem is that they believe what they say. This reverie talking, this constant undertone, or as some call it, speaking to oneself in the silence, is natural or self-hypnosis. More often than not, when one thinks, one talks. A microscopic movement of the larynx is known to occur during these silent undertones. Through these habitual thought and speaking patterns, one becomes programmed, or hypnotized to his own thinking. The result is simple: what goes in, comes out. Using the natural hypnosis process, and following the McClelland technique, a simple memory statement is offered, "My memory is improving each day, I see it happening and I am grateful." This brief statement, frequently repeated, will begin to express fully in one's life.[71]

4. Spaced Repetition, a memory tool and much more. This fourth and last area to be covered regarding memory is probably one of the most frequently used tools. Whenever the mind is bombarded with an idea, over and over, the mind finally becomes saturated with a new state of being. What is constantly repeated will be remembered. This has been stated earlier, but the focus here is specifically directed to memory. Returning now to the broader application of Spaced Repetition for idea embodiment, the third step in the Results Phase, the subject of habit, is covered as a by-product of the spaced repetition process.

Habit

Spaced repetition of words, actions, thoughts, even food rewards, will all develop into habits. The mind acts on the demands that are given it, and the body responds. There are both constructive habits and destructive habits. Habits are tools for living. They are formed for a purpose and they exist for a purpose. They maintain themselves for a purpose. But they do not always serve that purpose well.

Many "normal" people have habits which impede them, and actually diminish their happiness,

Results Phase

getting them into needless difficulties. Habits of procrastination, tardiness, timidity, hair-trigger temper, and the like, all begin as pieces of behavior. They can be treated as such, from the beginning, in the present moment. Habits are built-up little by little; spaced repetition means just that. Any habit may be refined, redirected or eliminated through the spaced repetition process. One's future does not depend upon the past. It depends upon the proper implementation of ideas already covered such as desire, imagery, and related Results Phase steps, along with focus on the area to be changed, and dedication and discipline to stand by until results are achieved.

It is true that most people form habits by discovering a method of solving a problem, a method of achieving a purpose, a method of obtaining satisfaction. The discovered method becomes standardized, i.e. habitual, because it is satisfactory, because it works well enough, or because it is the best method that can be found, even if it works badly. Any tool for living that is successful and satisfying, or which seems so, tends to create opportunities for its own use.[72] Such a person will tend to draw to him the submissive type individuals and if this continues, the person becomes the type who can't deal with anyone who can't be bossed.

For example, a young woman is brought up in a social environment where things are done for her, and at the same time she is not treated as an equal. As this woman grows older, she is discouraged from taking initiative; all details seem to be taken care of by someone else. In middle age she appears quite helpless. Budget, taxes, business matters, travel schedules, any decision, small or large, presents a problem for her. Although not pleased with this type of life, she is, in her own mind, behaving as she was taught in early life, and feels that this is the way a lady should behave: "I must be taken care of." This person has become a victim of habit; the habit of helplessness has crept into her life at an early age and it was never arrested.

Every habit, good or bad, is a standardized method for dealing with the problems of life; bad habits being unsatisfactory and disappointing methods, and good ones being staisfactory and rewarding methods. Every habit, too, is learned and established in the same way; namely, by discovering that it works, or at least seems to work, and then continuing the process through spaced repetition.

Spaced repetition, as used in the advertising media, is designed specifically to lead one to use a product with the purpose that a learned habit will be formed. The advertising industry plays upon the emotional nature of the individual, knowing fully that natural habit-forming tendencies exist. Awareness of consistent patterns in daily living and a present evaluation of current habits is recommended if positive changes are desired.

D. Individual Response and Self-Driven Results

These two categories are covered together, since they both relate to cause and effect. Individual response deals with inner self, while self-driven results deals with environmental factors. In both cases, it is universally accepted that a cause cannot be created without having a corresponding effect. Whether the discussion revolves around a physical condition of the body (physical disease), or has to do with one's environment (job status), the same conclusion can be reached, i.e., because there is a cause, there must be an effect.

Newton's third law of motion states that for every action, there is an equal and opposite reaction. This principle exists to be used or not be used, to be realized or be unrealized. However, the principle *is!* This principle may be used to great advantage for such purposes as rocket and jet transportation, or merely remain as words on the printed page. Both choices are available. In all honesty, the principle does not care about its utilization. It just exists!

The same is true in relation to the Results Phase. If the tools are used in a manner to enhance or elevate oneself toward better working conditions, receiving a pay raise, or even getting the boss's job (providing a better one for the boss is our only goal here), a corresponding effect or result will follow. Affecting the environment and creating a desire to do so is not as difficult as is commonly thought, once there is a basic understanding of how this is accomplished.

Without going into great detail, several areas will be covered here, clearly demonstrating the thought/response factor in the individual and the environment.

Individual Thought/Response Factor
Example 1. An individual is attending a social event and is discussing someone who is

not present. The conversation reaches a point where several unpleasant comments are made about the absent individual. The person making the comments suddenly notices the individual about whom he is speaking standing next to him within comfortable hearing range. Being startled at seeing this person so close, he becomes embarrassed and his face turns red.

Thought . . . The person heard what was said.

Response . . . Red face.

Example 2. While driving on an icy street, a young boy chasing a red rubber ball darts out in front of your car. You jam on the brakes and begin to slide. Your heart begins to beat faster, adrenalin begins to flow and the blood recedes from the head.

Thought . . . I'm out of control.

Response . . . Immediate physiological reaction.

Example 3. While attending a lecture, you are singled out by the speaker and asked to get up before the group to make a few statements. You are not a public speaker and you become nervous.

Thought . . . I must speak before the group.

Response . . . Cold hands, wet palms, butterflies in the stomach.

These are all examples of how an individual responds immediately to the thought process. It is clear that even if the individual involved does not physically act out the event, the body will still physiologically respond to the thought.

Self-Driven Results Factor
Example 1. A business client has been requesting attention and service from you, but you have neglected his requests. The client decides to use a competitor's product.
Thought . . . I have not provided good service.
Response . . . Client cancels contract.

Example 2. Someone in your office does an outstanding job. You notice this and you are the first to comment on the excellent performance. The message is received in a very positive manner, and the individual perceives your sincerity. The persons responds to you positively throughout the day.
Thought . . . I will tell him that he did a great job.
Reponse . . . I like him, he's a pretty good guy.

Example 3. You are told that you have just won a million dollar sweepstakes, and that you should come downtown to pick up your check. Those around you are aware that something positive has happened to you even without a word being spoken.
Thought . . . I feel like a winner.
Response . . . People greet me like I'm a winner.

The process through which everyone's surroundings are created begins with each individual thought. Think the thought, create the image, develop the feeling. The body responds, and the results in one's life are directly related to the thoughts that are predeterminedly selected. Why, then, would someone choose thoughts of guilt, sickness or despair, knowing full well that like attracts like? One reason is that the person does not want to take the time, nor invest the energy, to change.

This five-step process to self-driven results can be used with numerous variations, applied to relationships, finances, health and other success-directed goals. If a spark of desire exists, put the five-step process into action and observe the orderly fashion in which the new situation evolves. Remember, when nurturing a desire, the desire is aroused and moves toward things represented by ideas and mental pictures. The stronger and clearer the idea or mental picture, the stronger and more insistent the aroused desire.

If one wishes to determine the true value of a desire, the first acknowledgement should be to intuition. To consider one's own thoughts is often the best counsel. Feelings of guilt or enthusiasm are good indications whether the desired end should be pursued. If one is willing to pay the price, the desired fulfillment is always within reach. However, the price that must be paid may be too expensive, and often people settle for something much less. In reference to becoming an actor, Jack Lemmon stated that one should, "Go for the moon, and if you hit it, it's like lightning. If you don't go for it, you'll

Results Phase

probably be a good stock actor, but you won't get the lightning."

[29]Thomas Troward, *The Dore' Lectures* (New York: Dode, Mead & Co., 1951), p. 27.

[30]Douglas Dean and John Mihalasky, *Testing for Executive ESP* (San Francisco, CA: Psychic Magazine, vol. VI, No. 1. Dec. 1974), p. 21.

[31]James Grayson Bolen, Editor, *Profiles in Business* (San Francisco, CA: Psychic Magazine, vol. VI, No. 1. Dec. 1974), p. 27-33.

[32]Genevieve Behrend, *Your Invisible Power* (Marina Del Rey, CA: DeVorss & Co., 1976) p. 15.

[33]James Grayson Bolen, *Al Pollard Interview* (San Francisco, CA: Psychic Magazine, vol. VI, No. 1. Dec. 1974), p. 12.

[34]Mike Samuels and Nancy Samuels, *Seeing With The Mind's Eye* (New York: Random House Inc., 1975), p. 5.

[35]James Allen, *As A Man Thinketh* (Lexington, KY: Successful Achievement, Inc., 1971), p. 8.

[36]A Collection of Monthly Letters, *Of Interest to Executives* (Montreal, Quebec: The Royal Bank of Canada, 1955), p. 55.

[37]Wayne Dyer, *The Sky's The Limit* (New York: Simon and Schuster, 1980), p. 40.

[38]Mike Samuels and Nancy Samuels, *Seeing with the Mind's Eye* (New York: Random House Inc., 1975), p. 168.

[39]Wally Minto, *Results Book* (Salt Lake City, UT:Hawkens Publishing, Inc., 1976), p. 20.

[40]Maxwell Maltz, *The Magic Power of Self Image Psychology* (New Jersey: Prentice-Hall, Inc. 1964), p. 23.

[41]Hans Selye, *Stress Without Distress* (New York: Signet, 1974), p. 20.

[42]J. Allen Boon, *Kinship With All Life* (San Francisco, CA: Harper & Row, 1954), p. 9.

[43]Norman Cousins, *Anatomy of an Illness* (New York: W.W. Norton & Co., 1979), p. 34.

[44]Norman Cousins, *One Chance in 500 To Live* (The Saturday Evening Post, May, June 1977), p. 110.

[45]Robert Collier Page, *How To Lick Executive Stress* (New York: Cornerstone Library, 1961), p. 13.

[46]James Melton, *Your Right to Fly* (Milwaukee, WI: Global Publications, 1978), p. 113.

[47]James L. Mursell, *How to Make and Break Habits* (Philadelphia, PA: J. B. Lippencott, Co., 1953), p. 73.

[48]Bormann, Howell, Nichols, Shapiro, *Interpersonal Communication in the Modern Organization* (New Jersey: Prentice-Hall, Inc. 1969), p. 268-273.

[49]Alexander Leafl, *Search for the Oldest People* (National Geographic, vol. 143, No. 1. January 1973), p. 99.

[50]Norman Cousins, *Anatomy of an Illness* (New York: W.W. Norton & Co., 1979), p. 17.

[51]Norman Cousins, *Anatomy of an Illness* (New York: W.W. Norton & Co., 1979), p. 55.

[52]C. Norman Shealy, *The Pain Game* (Millbrea, CA: Celestial Arts, 1976), p. 13.

[53]Simonton, Simonton and Creighton, *Getting Well Again* (Los Angeles, CA: J.P. Tarcher, Inc., 1978), p. 121.

[54]Simonton, Simonton and Creighton, *Getting Well Again* (Los Angeles, CA: J.P. Tarcher, Inc., 1978), p. 20.

[55]Barbara Brown, *New Mind, New Body* (New York: Harper & Row, 1974), p. 22.

[56]Simonton, Simonton and Creighton, *Getting Well Again* (Los Angeles, CA: J.P. Tarcher, Inc., 1978), p. 27.

[57]Mike Samuels and Nancy Samuels, *Seeing With the Mind's Eye* (New York: Random House Inc., 1975), p. 227.

[58]Simonton, Simonton and Creighton, *Getting Well Again* (Los Angeles, CA: J.P. Tarcher, Inc., 1978), p. 29.

[59]Arthur Deikman, *The Nature of Human Consciousness* (San Francisco, CA: W.H. Freeman & Co., 1968), p. 69-70.

[60]David P. Nowlis and Joe Kamiya, *The Nature Of Human Consciousness* (San Francisco, CA: W.H. Freeman & Co., 1968), p. 393-394.

[61]Hebert Benson, *The Relaxation Response* (New York: William Morrow & Co., Inc., 1975), p. 64.

[62]Yogi Tamachataka, *Science of Breath* (Chicago, IL: Yogi Publication Society, 1904), p.10.

[63]Mike Samuels and Nancy Samuels, *Seeing With The Mind's Eye* (New York: Random House Inc., 1975), p. 121.

[64]Mike Samuels and Nancy Samuels, *Seeing With the Mind's Eye* (New York: Random House Inc., 1975). Vernon Howard, *Psycho-Pictography* (New York: Parker Publishing Co., Inc., 1965). Maxwell Maltz, *The Magic Power of Self-Image Psychology* (New Jersey: Prentice-Hall, Inc. 1964).

[65]Maxwell Maltz, *The Magic Power of Self-Image Psychology* (New Jersey: Prentice-Hall, Inc. 1964), p.26.

[66]Hugo A. Bedau, *Making Decisions* (Reading, MA: Addison-Wesley Pub., Co., 1978), p. 39.

Results Phase

[67]Ronald H. Bailey, *The Role of the Brain* (New York: Time-Life Books, 1975), p. 74.

[68]Ronald H. Bailey, *The Role of the Brain* (New York: Time-Life Books, 1975), p. 95.

[69]Bernard C. Gindes, *New Concepts of Hypnosis* (Hollywood, CA: Wilshire Book Company, 1951), p. 59.

[70]David B. Cheek and Leslie M. LeCron, *Clinical Hypnotherapy* (New York: Grune & Stratton, 1968), p. 63.

[71]Donald Curtis, *Human Problems and How to Solve Them* (New Jersey: Prentice-Hall, Inc., 1962), p. 19.

V

Acquiring Skills

Acquiring Skills

Preliminary Considerations

Thus far, the reader has explored some of the major areas that must be present for Vital Enthusiasm to become an active part of his daily life. Focused Vital Enthusiasm is a basic building block in forming a solid foundation for individual achievement. Any result is largely determined by effort. It is commonly known that thought determines what is desired, but action determines what is achieved.

A guideline for the implementation process is offered here, but before presenting some specific physical tools for tapping and channeling Vital Enthusiasm, the reader is asked to consider the following: a major block against the expression of Vital Enthusiasm is admiration or condemnation of others. This may startle the reader, especially with regard to admiration. It should be noted, however, that focusing on the positive and negative qualities of others limits one's own power to achieve; but this, too, has its roots in the self-image concept. The introduction of this thought is to reinforce the no-limit self-image concept one must hold if true expression of Vital Enthusiasm is to be achieved.

Observation vs. Opposition

People are often quick to point out specific qualities in others without realizing that these very same qualities may exist within themselves. Such qualities can be either positive or negative. Like tends to attract like. Insight for personal growth may be gained from this phenomenon by observing those people who comprise a large portion of one's time, and then by considering their comments, activities and interests. This must be done without judgment, but with awareness that much may be learned from such individuals.

Without usually realizing it, people generally tend to see in others qualities that lie deeply within themselves. Other people mirror traits that are either liked or disliked. The basic fact is that a quality, characteristic, attitude or talent that is strongly liked or disliked in someone else, is innately carried in oneself. Upon casual observation, undesirable traits may be noticed in someone else. This does not necessarily mean that the observer carries these negative points within himself at a conscious level, since they are only observations of someone else and may not reflect strong emotion. There is a distinct difference between observation and opposition, i.e., between acknowledgement and resistance. When a quality in another is strongly resisted, more likely than not that same quality exists within the person resisting and, therefore, he should look deeply within to better understand the nature of the resistance. Any person who desires positive change should not resist or suppress any negative trait, for by doing so, the individual is only masking an area requiring attention.

Close observation of friends and loved ones should provide a real picture of one's own thinking. The general tendency is to attract people who think in similar fashions. Cultivating relationships with people whom one admires and who have qualities that one wishes to develop can be helpful for personal growth. Learning from others through observation and without judgment, then, provides for a higher form of education. Cultivating this talent is an elevating process.[73]

Observations by Others

Every individual should pay careful heed to any critical comments, suggestions, or hints that others may give about individual behavior. Often others can see into a personality in a way that may not be perceived by the individual himself. It is not wise to brush off these opinions when they are made apparent. Not often will a person receive temperate, well-considered and explicit criticism from a friend. If, by good fortune, such criticism is offered, it should be accepted as a valuable gift. As with any such gift, it should be thought over with the utmost care and on

Acquiring Skills

a deeper level, taken to heart, even if, on reflection, it cannot be wholly agreed upon. But above all, it should not be brushed off as insignificant.

Corrective criticism is often brushed off, but in more cases than not, it is greeted with a first reaction of anger. Many people actually fly into a rage and repudiate what is said about them with violent words, thinking they have been openly insulted. Most often, revenge is taken subconsciously by inwardly discrediting the critic, which is a way of striking back, i.e., by disregarding what has been said. Do not discount criticism too quickly, for most likely an unrecognized distasteful behavior pattern is the cause.

It is not advisable to rely chiefly on careful, well-considered criticisms that are presented in a well-meaning fashion. Such criticisms are rare. Valuable insights may be gained regarding personal conduct from direct hints and suggestions or even unintentional intimations. The tone of another's voice, significant hesitations, a meaningful glance are all examples of communications and often reveal a great deal about personal perceptions. It is a great mistake to always be on the look-out for adverse criticism, or to be overly concerned with impressions that are being made. But an even greater mistake is to be insensitive about the effect of one's behavior pattern on other people or to their opinions. The important consideration is not the view or immediate impression that another may hold. The important consideration is to see oneself more clearly in the light of other people's reaction.

Again, as Emerson put it: "First, be a good

animal." Pay particular heed to the reactions of naive and simple people, children, and even animals. A child often reveals something about an individual that is very startling, and the revelation may be extremely beneficial. Within certain limits, children see very clearly, and conventions do not prevent them from expressing themselves. Because of this level of candor, a flash of insight may reveal some disconcerting things about one's own mental make-up.

In addition to outside observation, observe your own stream of consciousness by becoming consciously aware of the general trend of your thinking. Taking stock of thoughts, ideas, impressions, likes, dislikes and other feelings that flow through the mind provides a general overview of one's basic consciousness. When the stream of consciousness is recognized, the focusing process may begin.

Focus

A scattered mind produces scattered results. A focused mind produces an inner state of order that naturally leads to the steps necessary to bridge the gap between *wanting* and *having*. (See figure 5).

People tend to equate the quality of focus with the powers of concentration. Although focus and concentration do align themselves closely in many areas, for the purpose of Vital Enthusiasm they must be expressed differently. Anyone can force his mind, at the exclusion of all else, to concentrate on a specific area. The length of time in which this can be achieved will depend on the mental training of the

Focus · Goals · Organization · Habits · Action

(Figure 5/Bridging the Gap)

individual. However, this is more in the form of willpower, and is not the type of focus that is desirable for the ultimate manifestation of one's goal. Willpower is meant to be used as a decision-making tool and not for any long-term purpose. This may be equated with flexing the muscles for an indefinite period of time which cannot, and should not, be done. To force things to become that which, by their very nature, they are not, is to digress rather than progress. Success depends on using, and not opposing, natural laws.

A let-it-be, as opposed to make-it-happen attitude should be incorporated into focused thought, an attitude, not of control, but of ease. A focused mind is a way of listening more deeply, listening to the inner mind as the thoughts flow in and out. Observing the stream of consciousness and passing no judgment, while holding a non-resistant attitude, is the right kind of focus. A quiet inner contemplation of one's desire, as an accomplished fact, carries strength. Care must be taken during such contemplation not to exert strenuous effort. Instead of effort, contemplation should be accomplished by a feeling of pleasure and restfulness in foreseeing the accomplishment of one's desires.

Hatha Yoga, Transcendental Meditation and other disciplines advocate a focused mind, but the process is a mechanical one. Focus evolving from true desire allows individuals the freedom to explore the innermost parts of the mind, the freedom to learn and to watch with interest those activities which make up the total individual. This is accomplished in a way that does not interfere with, but instead, expands the individual idea-gathering capabilities of the mind. A focused mind is an astonishingly alert mind; it is a mind that is aware of every thought and every feeling, never judging right or wrong, but just watching the thought process and moving with it. Some may call this a form of meditation, but often the word meditation gets confused with a definite form of Eastern philosophy.[74] Although the Eastern form is more formal, neither is difficult. Desire will bring forth a focused mind. Burning desire will color all experiences in life with a single purpose, whether walking, riding a bus, resting or anything else.

There is no educational requirement or aptitude necessary to experience a focused mind. Desire is the sole ingredient needed. Just as each person experiences fear, anger, contentment and excitement, so does each person contain all that is necessary to call into being the focused mind. With the focused mind, a heightened sense of alertness can be realized, making each successive step toward goal realization progressively easier.

In dealing with the substance of things not seen, a state of mind must be attained. In such a state the ultimate reality is seen and felt. The individual must realize that in dealing with this intangible substance, mental manipulation is, in reality, the actual point of origin of the desire, even though in a different mode than formally acknowledged.

Those whose mental bias is toward physical science recognize this law of mental manipulation as the creative force throughout all nature. And those who have a mathematical inclination might reflect that all solids are generated from the movement of a point, which, as Euclid states, is that which has no parts or magnitude, and therefore is as complete an abstraction as any non-physical nucleus could be.[75] Mental creations must be regarded as non-physical realities and their manifestations must be trusted implicitly.

Life Management Plan

Planning for a vacation is a common occurrence, even if a one-day vacation. Most people plan extensively where they will go, what sights to see, what highway to take and exactly how far they will travel each day. They figure out how much time they have to spend, and then proportion their trip accordingly to return on a certain day. It is amazing that most people take more time planning their summer vacation than they do in planning their lives. A positive plan of action to reach a goal can be a key instrument to achieving success.

If someone were asked what they were doing in life to plan for failure, they would most likely say, "I'm not planning for failure, I'm planning for success." Next, when asked what their plan is, they will be hard pressed for an answer. Research indicates that for every hundred people, only one actually has written goals. A survey conducted found that, by age 65:

    1 in a hundred would be rich;
    4 would be financially independent;
    5 would still be working because they have to;
    54 would be broke;
    36 would be dead.

It appears that only about one percent of the population has written goals. Clearly, most people do not plan for the future.

Certainly the greater majority of people do not consciously plan for failure in life, but the irony is that by not planning, failure is often the result. It is known that most people by the age of 65 are dependent upon someone else for support. It all looks good while still young, and even during mid-life, but suddenly the realization comes that planning for the later years has not been done. It has been said so often that if one does not have a direction in mind, the destination reached will be uncertain. Even if a goal is set, the lack of self-discipline is often one of the major factors involved in failure. Thus, a habit is formed of letting oneself down, and the familiar trap of getting sidetracked is accepted. In either case, it is a blow to self-esteem, and each instance helps to build a failure pattern. It seems that successful people tend to form habits that unsuccessful people don't. Individual effectiveness may be increased tremendously by utilizing a life plan.

Many people have said that as long as they have a roof over their head, clothes to wear, and food to eat, they are happy. Certainly this is more a figure of speech than an actuality. These same persons, if given a chance to win a million-dollar sweepstakes, might very well look at their home and say, "We can't live in a shack like this." They would walk into their garage, look at their automobile and say, "How can the governor of this state allow anyone to drive in a deathtrap like this; we need a new car." What is the difference between two individuals — one without, and one with, a million dollars? The difference is primarily based upon belief. However, belief is not to be confused with the normal change that occurs when an individual suddenly becomes a millionaire, e.g., changes in value systems, etc.

Another example. What if someone said that somewhere in the state, buried three feet beneath the surface of the earth, lies a million dollars? Few would be motivated enough to dig up an entire state. However, if a certified geologist told you that a lode deposit existed in your front yard, you would immediately start digging. The difference is obviously belief. The degree of accomplishment depends somewhat upon the degree of belief. Thus, if a believable plan is designed, one has a better opportunity of achieving the desired end result. With this in mind, the 7+1 Life Management Plan was designed.

The 7+1 Life Management Plan

I. Write your goal down.

It is important to bring your desire into the physical world by actually writing it on a piece of paper. This is the beginning step and may seem insignificant, but it is important. Many people say that they have their goal so firmly planted in their mind that they do not have to write it down — write it down anyway. By formalizing the desire on paper, you can become very creative and the focusing process is, again, put into action. There are people who are paid highly to simply sit and write down ideas. When the mind is focused on a particular area, one tends to become very creative. The mind works best within some limitation. If someone says: "Think of something nice," the answer might be: "A nice what? There are many nice things." But if someone were to say: "Think about something nice about your face." Now the task becomes more clear, e.g., the face has character, has intriguing eyes and displays warmth. The mind tends to zero in on the area of attention. Writing a goal down will not only promote expansion of the idea, but also will assist in clarifying the purpose.

Acquiring Skills

II. Be specific.

Being specific is important. It would be foolish, for example, to walk into a restaurant and say, "Give me some food." The importance of being specific is obvious. The same holds true when requesting airline tickets: airline tickets to where? Without specifics, any goal is elusive. Take the desire for a specific sum of money, say $5,000 or $10,000. Many individuals say that laying claim to a specific amount of money limits them, but this is not really the case. Claiming a specific amount makes the demonstration both easier and more rapid. Actually, one is not limited by making a claim to a specific amount because the principle can be applied and reapplied an endless number of times, either in succession or concurrently. Many goals may be worked on at the same time and limits should not be self-imposed. Whatever can be conceived can come into being through an orderly process.

Some people say that they would like happiness and peace of mind for their goal. Eleanor Roosevelt said that happiness and peace of mind were not goals in themselves; rather, she said that happiness and peace of mind were the results of goals. Being specific is a key ingredient to the successful fulfillment of a goal.

In homes for the aged, the death rate drops drastically just before special events such as birthdays, weddings, Christmas, anniversaries and the like. Why is this? It seems that many set a goal to live at least one more anniversary, birthday or Christmas. Having something to live for makes life more valuable. For anything to become a reality, the desire must be clearly stated. Certainly there are activities, thoughts and material items which people are not specific about, but by clearly stating their desires, and committing them to paper, the opportunity for their goals to become a reality is greatly enhanced. Like a target market for an advertising campaign, first the market is determined, then plans are made to impact that area. The same principles apply to an individual moving toward a specific goal.

III. Set a date.

Set the actual date that a goal is to be achieved. Mark the date on the calendar. Often people resist marking the calendar for they fear they will not reach it, and failing to achieve means just plain failure. This is when they come down with "tomorrowitis": "I'll do it tomorrow." If one says he will do it tomorrow, what is really being said is that it will not be accomplished today. Most people have been, at one time or another, on a diet, either to gain or to lose weight. The best time to begin a diet always seems to be tomorrow, or Monday, or the sixth Monday of next month. Of course, people often slip back into their old ways sometime on Tuesday, and for some reason, they cannot possibly start the diet again until next Monday, a week later. New Year's resolutions pose a similar challenge. Often by noon of Jan. 1, the dieter has already been defeated.

Of course, this gives the individual another year to procrastinate, for what would be the sense in beginning a New Year's resolution on Jan. 2? Sad as it is, individuals often accept behavior from themselves that they would not tolerate from others. For example, a friend telephones and would like to meet for breakfast tomorrow. Your friend wants to have breakfast about 7:00 a.m. and this means that you will have to get up about 6:00 a.m. You arrive at the specified restaurant and wait, 7:15, 7:30, and your friend doesn't show up. Upon returning home, your friend calls to tell you that he got tied up and couldn't make it. He apologizes and asks you to meet him tomorrow morning at the same time. You agree. Tomorrow morning, the same thing happens. Upon returning home, he calls and makes another excuse. The request is made to meet again, but this time you are quite skeptical.

How long should this manipulation be allowed to continue? Not many people would offer a third chance to the friend, and some probably would not even have given a second chance. Often behavior is accepted from oneself that would not be accepted from his best friend. A decision is made to start on a diet, improve the business, give more time to the children, make more money, or start a physical health program. Yet when rising the next morning, with a perfectly straight face, "tomorrow" echoes loudly. It has been said that character is the ability to follow through on a good resolution long after the mood in which it was made has passed. Of course, the biggest mistake of all is to do nothing. It is far better to try to do something great and fail, than to do nothing and succeed. For everything that is desired, something must be given. When setting a financial goal, consideration might include giving away an extra hour at home so that an additional sales call could be made. Rising one hour earlier than usual each morning would provide nine extra 40-hour weeks each year. By eliminating alcoholic beverages at lunchtime, afternoons will be more productive. Giving up leisure time to upgrade one's education in the present job, or to cultivate another, is something to be considered. Social involvements might be evaluated as time spent toward attaining a goal.

Any serious goal demands change of some kind. Without change, experiences are repeated. Often people claim that they would really like to reach a particular goal, but that time just doesn't permit, or that something else got in the way. Here, the desire to achieve is probably not significant enough; with strong desire, these blocks can normally be overcome. A time frame and commitment to a specific date will provide guidelines for the speed with which the goal is to be attained. The method of accomplishment can then be constructed.

IV. Visualize the end result.

Think of the end result of any desire in terms of a present posssibility. Visualize the goal in the mind to create a mental image. Review of the visualization section may be helpful; it clearly describes the techniques, as well as reasons, for the visualization process.

Seeing one's dreams become a reality is not uncommon. The statement, "I have a dream," has been heard many times. Whether building a business, realizing the construction of a home, or setting a nation's sights on reaching the moon as John F. Kennedy did in the early 1960s, visualization of a dream is paramount. A historian once stated: "Where there is no vision the people will perish."

Moving confidently in the direction of dreams

and desires allows the natural visualization process the freedom of growth. Confident visualizations carry with them the strength to pursue predetermined goals. Fears, doubts, anxieties and self-defeating behaviors also carry with them the capacity of materialization. Anything that is feared or revered will be attracted like a magnet. Feelings generate and expand the visualizations created in the mind so it helps to develop the art of thinking big. Constant reminders, such as visual representations of goals posted in the home, the office or the automobile, keep the dream fresh and exciting, while building a firm, feeling foundation toward future achievement.

Most important is to keep an image firmly planted in the mind, paying careful attention to detail and repetition. Focus and intensity of thought will result in physical realization of a dream desired. As in *Man of La Mancha*, "This is my dream, this is my quest . . ." Visualization concepts are simple and, when used properly, are extremely effective. The ability to visualize an end result must be challenged by individual experimentation, i.e., by individual trial and error.

V. List the benefits.

Many people stop short of step five, but this is a most important factor in reaching a goal. Focusing on this area will make the goal more clear so its final realization can be more positively accepted. Almost any desire may be achieved if the proper steps toward its realization are taken. Many people do not believe this because they have trouble believing they can have what is justifiably attainable. By listing benefits, the visualization process is stimulated causing positive thought patterns to form. Habit also plays an important role in goal-setting. This will be covered in greater detail under the section, "Habits For Success."

VI. List the detriments.

Write down what it will mean to you if the goal is not reached. Some people may look at this as a negative approach, but in reality, it is quite a logical step, for both positive and negative aspects of a situation are generally considered before a decision is made. By listing detriments, fears are placed out in the open. The challenge is to evaluate them, thus gaining better understanding of which direction to take. One noted American psychologist said that unrest, unhappiness and uneasiness in the world today is caused by people living far below their capacity. If we plan on being anything less than we are capable, we will probably be unhappy all our lives. We either move forward into growth or we step backward into sameness. Often individuals become satisfied with a particular position in life because it is easy and a change would be uncomfortable. Although not happy, complacency sets in, and the decision to remain status quo is made. Change sometimes means confronting oneself with the possibility of criticism, failure, and even success. Sometimes the fear of criticism is stronger than the desire for success. Too often people put the opinions of others above their own opinions. In a world that is doing its best to mold lives into sameness, it is the unique individual who continues to strive toward constructive nonconformity.

Realizing that negative aspects will continue to

persist, to irritate, or even to develop, combined with non-achievement, depression is sometimes a negative stimulus. Discontent breeds growth, and change is only possible when the need for change is acknowledged. Change for the mere sake of change is never good, but change directed toward fulfillment can be a strong motivating factor.

VII. Make the decision.

After listing all the benefits and all the detriments involved in a goal, a decision must be made and a plan must be designed. This is done in almost every area of life. When buying a home, the qualities will be reviewed and a decision will be made. Likewise with an automobile, one evaluates such variables as mileage, luggage space, interior room, cost, interest rates, etc. When entering into a marriage or a new job position, the positives should be studied as well as the negatives. Weighing both sides of the issue and making a decision to advance toward the goal ignites the spark needed to reach the end result. Decisiveness in setting goals, as in most areas of life, is critical to success. It is better to make a wrong decision than to make no decison at all. Indecison is fatal.

VIII. Act silently.

The importance of this area demands a number-one status, thus, the 7 + 1 plan. The old saying, "Go and tell no man," means to remain quiet regarding one's inner desires, thereby maintaining a high level of inner excitement and inner enthusiasm. If a steam engine continually blows its whistle while climbing a mountain, it soon does not have enough power to complete the climb. When a goal is held confidently, quietly and surely the goal tends to manifest itself. Movement and direction through life is visible because of accomplishments, not words. Remaining quiet about a goal helps build enthusiasm. Premature verbalization of one's plans can cause them to dematerialize, even if a portion of the final plan has already been accomplished. Speak only with those who support your goal. Positive reassurance is supportive, but even this must be closely guarded or the energy already developed through the previous seven-step process may be diminished. Tell the world, but show it first! The true measure of a man's worth is not in what he said he would do, but, rather, in what he accomplished.

Organization

Basically, organization boils down to "who does what when." There are several decision steps involved in every good organization plan. They consist of:[76]

1. Determining the work or activities necessary to be performed for the implementation of a particular plan. The things to be done or tasks to be performed become duties.

2. Next, these activities are grouped into positions so they can be assigned to an individual, thus becoming responsibilities.

3. Then, authority is assigned to each position, conferring on the person holding the position the right to carry out the responsibilities himself, or to order others to carry them out.

Note that authority and power differ in that

power refers to the ability to get things done, either personally, or by commanding or influencing others to do them. A person may develop power through respect, knowledge, judgment, seniority, age, former accomplishments, fear, or various other qualities. Authority, on the other hand, if it is not respected, will command little or no power. An executive who recognizes the value of good organization and wants to support the management system, unless he also has the required authority for his actions, is careful not to exercise power derived from seniority or popularity.

4. The next step in organizational planning is to determine authority relationships among positions. That is, decide who reports to whom and what kind of authority, if any, the holder of each position may exercise. This will ensure that every person knows who his superiors are, who his subordinates are, and what type and extent of authority may be exercised.

5. Finally, the personal qualifications required for superior performance in each position should be decided, e.g., duties, responsibilities, authorities, relationships, and personal requirements of positions. This kind of planning harnesses and legitimizes power. It also helps to contain illegitimate power.

Most likely, once the ideal organizational plan has been developed, difficulty in finding the ideal person or persons to fill the positions will be encountered. But it is better to accept compromises in an ideal plan than not to have an ideal plan from which to start.

Time Management

Job description and delegation play a key role in time management. Many do not realize that through the proper organization of time, tasks can be accomplished efficiently and effectively. A balance in "doing" is needed. Thus, sometimes it becomes necessary to step back and look at the total picture, and only then move forward again to complete the task. There is a time for engagement and a time for withdrawal, a time to just walk around the job and think about it, and a time to just laugh at it.[77] Being in a hurry can be a detriment. There is a difference between hurrying and working rapidly. The old adage "haste makes waste" is true. Speed can be equated with efficiency, but hurrying generally does not fit the same category. The story of the medical intern and the master surgeon makes this quite clear.

The intern and master surgeon were in the operating room and the master surgeon said to the young intern: "We'll have to cut this area, lift the heart aside, get to the problem area and replace the heart. All of this will have to be done within forty-five seconds." The intern was concerned and said: "But doctor, will we have enough time?" The surgeon replied: "We'll have plenty of time, just as long as we don't hurry."

Over-Organization

Becoming overly organized is as detrimental as being unorganized; it can be an effectiveness killer.[78] Often, people spend so much time getting organized that they do not leave time to actually do the job they have set out to do. Keeping lists, clearing the desk, paying too much attention to minute details and running around with a stopwatch can can create big problems. Here again, balance is suggested. Many activities such as these are time robbers. Other time-robbers, stemming from under-organization, or over-organization, are interruptions, such as unscheduled visitors, telephone calls, too much paper work, or time spent communicating with subordinates and co-workers. All these are essentially symptoms of being unorganized, but they are not really a basic problem. Most people simply do not have their priorities in order. When asked what is the most annoying thing on the job, many will immediately reply, "interruptions." However, it would be foolish to suggest that one unplug the telephone, lock the door and leave word that one absolutely does not want to be disturbed. The telephone is needed and communication with the staff and clients is necessary; this interaction is critical to business decision-making.[79]

Priorities

Interruptions are generally a result of seeing people who shouldn't be seen, or spending too much time on items that do not relate to predetermined goals. In short, priorities have not been established. To become efficient and effective in work, it is necessary to be specific about the intended order of accomplishments, i.e., A, B, and C. Everything can be broken down into a category which is, in itself, easier to handle, such as sales calls, filing, reports, even the pile of papers on the desk. Sort the pile of paper into three piles: A, B, and C. The most important items into pile A, the less urgent in B, and the lowest priority item in the C pile. Handle the A's at once. At least begin them. Even if the task is long and involved, the idea of beginning, making a dent in it, is important. One is more apt to continue something that has been started than to undertake something that has been lying dormant for a period of time, because it then becomes what is often looked upon as a dreaded task. The B category should be handled when there is time. Items in the category are important, but their completion is not immediately necessary. Finally, the C category is placed in a file cabinet, drawer, or some other location that is out of sight. Be aware of their location when asked to produce these items, but when the drawer is full, most of it can be thrown away without really missing a thing.

"If something needs to be done, give it to a busy person," is sound advice. Busy people are usually organized, they set priorities, and things get accomplished. Obviously this does not apply to those who work hard at looking busy. Everyone lives a total of 168 hours a week, and no matter how it is spent, everyone has exactly the same amount of time to work with; that is all there is. Yet many people complain about a lack of time — simply because they have not learned to use it wisely. One simple rule is to handle each piece of paper only once. Don't put down an incoming letter or memo that requires review or response until the matter has been attended. Most often, it is easier to think of a reply when a response is fresh in the mind. If the matter requires more thought than an on-the-spot decision, take the first step toward completion, get an opinion of another, make the telephone call to get the project rolling, but do something other than just put it back in the pile of incoming papers.

Tools

Using the proper tools can also be a time-saver. Tools of a trade vary from the accountant's pencil and worksheets, to the chemist's glass beaker — and everything in between. The proper tools are essential for efficient completion of a job.

An investment at the start of a project, both in time to survey the tools needed, and in dollars to buy the needed equipment or supplies, will be well worth it in the long run. Many a job has been abandoned due to short tempers, hurt feelings and even for health reasons, because the proper tools were not on the list of priorities. It has been said that the difference in wise men and fools is often found in their choice of tools.

Space

Space organization is another area that sometimes gets put aside due to an unawareness of its importance. Space organization deals not only with the immediate working area, but also the general area. A cluttered desk, room, automobile, closet, even the garments that are worn, all can cause a cluttered result in a project. If allowed to continue, the result may influence one's general work pattern, and unfavorable habit patterns will be formed. Once formed, they are difficult to remove (see section on Habits For Success). Don't be fooled by the executive who keeps a cluttered desk to give the appearance of being busy. This is analagous to one who frantically manufactures artificial activities to give the illusion of happiness. Frantically manufacturing clutter does not make one busy. A desk piled high with papers may give such an impression, but it is not necessarily the case. The reverse may also be true. A spotless desk, room, or working area can indicate that more time is spent on cleaning than on working. Returning to the statement: "Everything in moderation," makes sense. Probably the handiest desk item could be the "in" and "out" boxes. The key here is to move the items from one box to another — in to out! If this is not done, the tendency is to let the "in" box pile up, and take care of other things.

Eighty-Twenty

The 80/20 rule seems to apply almost everywhere. Eighty percent of one's business is developed from 20 percent of the clients. Eighty percent of the telephone calls come from 20 percent of the callers. Eighty percent of one's time is spent working to achieve the 20 percent leisure time. The same relates to studying a foreign language: 80 percent of those who have studied a foreign language in high school go on to further foreign language study, while less than 20 percent of those without this experience elect foreign language during their college careers.[80] The

Acquiring Skills

80/20 rule is prevalent through life, right down to making a "to do" list. If all the things one wants to do are weighed according to their value, 80 percent of the value will come from only 20 percent of the items. It makes sense, then, that if one's "to do" list contains 10 items, then 20 percent, or two of those items, will produce the most value. Thus, it would be wise to locate those two items, tag them A's, and get them done. Even if they are time-consuming, more value is often received from doing them, than tackling the entire list, one to 10. Chances are, if the other eight items do not get done until the next day, it won't matter anyway.

Things I'll Do Today

The most common name for a "things to be done" list is a "To Do" list. Consider changing the name to "Things I'll Do Today." The concept comes from the idea that what is planted into the mind and repeated over and over will eventually get done. With this in mind, begin a list. But do not become burdened with too many items. Ten would be good for one day. The reason for this is simple. If 10 items are completed in one day, the entire list has been accomplished and a feeling of success is experienced. If 20 items are on the list and only 15 of them are completed, one feels defeated, and a sense of failure ensues.

Most people, when asked what to list on their daily program, will list business calls, washing, dusting, meetings, contract closings, or whatever else applies in routine life. A daily list, however, must also include items for the complete person, and this is where most people fall short. Items such as jogging, resting, think time, time with the children and family, as well as work items, should be included in the list of "Things I'll Do Today!"

Procrastination

Procrastination is a sure way to avoid today. It is a delusion entered into in a self-convincing manner, giving special dispensation for non-action. Many work under the assumption that things will get better, or that something can be finished, or started, later. This is a way of not admitting that a job will probably not get done. It is a mask, individually designed, to cover a variety of non-action behaviors. Postponement without guilt, upset or anxiety would allow the present moment to be experienced more freely. This, however, is not often the case.

Procrastination comes in varying degrees. For instance, a poor job can be explained easily. The excuse might be used that there was not enough time to complete the job properly when, in fact, plenty of time was available; it just was not used efficiently. Waiting until the last minute, with the excuse that one works best under pressure, usually results in something less than top performance.

Identifying Procrastination

There are many ways to identify procrastination. Some of these are:
  • Wishing or hoping for some big deal to fall

into one's life is one of the most popular versions. Thinking that a big breakthrough, personal change, or management change will prove to be the panacea, is common.

• Realizing the need and practicality to correct one's health, but not taking action, is an area many have discovered. Overeating, smoking, excessive drinking of alcoholic beverges, realizing the need for exercise, all these are things known, but seldom acted upon.

• Another sign of procrastination is desiring to relocate and waiting for the "right" time. Certainly there are times when it may be easier to take action than others, but in general, if someone is really serious about making a change, it should not be put off.

• Hanging on to a relationship, and simply hoping for an improvement, is usually fruitless. Here again, action is necessary to bring about change. By procrastinating, the inevitable is only delayed. Correcting a situation at its inception is usually easier than after it has developed deep roots in the life pattern.

• Delaying the little things by putting them aside for another day, thinking they are unimportant and may go away, can make them develop into virtual monsters. Sometimes by doing some of the little things, i.e., the phone call, letter response, getting the new shoestring, relaxes the mind, thus allowing more mental freedom for a greater challenge.

• Excessive planning is also a procrastination tool. Pre-planning, planning, post-planning: "Let's do anything so we don't have to start." The importance of a solid plan for later implementation is not to be discounted, however, there are limits. Sometimes, the course of action can not be determined until the process has begun. Excessive planning may be rooted deeper than one might think, and it could stem from a strong need to achieve, without having the self-confidence to move directly toward the goal.

• To live vicariously through others is another form of procrastination. Often parents will find themselves leading a life essentially through their children. Their happiness seems to be gained only through the activities of their children. Using the child as a ploy, although unintenional as it may be, an individual has again created a non-action status. Vicarious living is experienced often through entertainers. An individual may place himself mentally in someone's situation, thereby partially fulfilling a need for achievement. Vicarious management is similar, often causing non-action.

Ignoring areas that need attention is still another. It is true that everything passes in time, but the success-oriented person acts with a total plan, moving toward a goal in a complete fashion, i.e., with a well-desired plan.

Boredom is procrastination and a sure sign of putting things off. Boredom is created and experienced only through the eyes of the boring. Life is filled with challenges to discover and experience. There is no boring person, town, or job; everything is of an inner creation, and if one keeps the mind alert and active, boredom will not be a part of his life. There are many reasons why people procrastinate. Consider the following:

Acquiring Skills

• The great escape, the ultimate fantasy. Fooling oneself by believing that the task will get done; buying time, or so it seems, when, in reality, time is actually lost to complete the stated aim. Procrastination is a false escape, but it is a major reason that many people subconsciously use.

• Everyone likes to be considered a doer. Procrastination permits this delusion. By saying that a task will be done, in a convincing manner, silently and to others, the action process can be avoided. What is often forgotten is that individuals are not judged by their words, but by their actions and accomplishments.

• Fear of change. Change is often difficult, but non-change means non-growth. To be alive and not to grow is a contradiction. A flower that is alive is growing; a flower that is not growing is dying. If one is alive, one is growing. Life means growth, and growth means change. To fear change is fruitless, for change is the only thing that is constant in life. Realizing this makes it easier to handle the varying degrees of change, making them less fearful.

• It's their fault. Often people are too quick to point fingers, blaming others for what is, in reality, their own doing. It is always easier to place the cause of a particular situation externally than to admit personal responsibility. This is most certainly true with respect to an undesirable encounter. Everyone has seen people take credit where credit is due when the situation is favorable. Statements like: "I'm a self-made person, I created my success," are common. But the reverse is seldom heard: "I'm a self-made failure, I created this mess and I'm responsible." Usually, the accusing finger points at the crowd, charging all "those people" with the wrong, never realizing that the real problem lies deep within the accusing individual.

- The economy! Has the economy ever been good? Waiting to buy, sell, invest, save, change jobs, the list is endless. Waiting until the economy improves before a move is made is like waiting for Prince Charming. Money has been placed as a barrier in many peoples lives, when, in fact, money really is not the problem. One hundred-thousand dollars could be given to everyone on this planet this very instant — and by midnight some would be rich and some would be poor. It is not how much money one has, but, rather, the level of consciousness one has reached. "Money seems to come around to see what kind of a fellow you are," is an appropriate adage.

Procrastination Elimination

- Cut major tasks into as many small, manageable segments as possible. When time permits, accomplish one of these small segments. Sometimes, long-term projects overpower a person to a point where he feels helpless. Short segment achievement allows for a feeling of accomplishment, as well as putting a dent in a big ominous job.
- Obtain a DIN degree. Do it now! Waiting for a specific date is another form of procrastination. By tackling a certain project now, rather than waiting for a specific date, the habit of taking the plunge is formed; operate on a "now" basis of living. The "doer" consciousness is established not only in one's own mind, but also in others. This will be reflected

also in the attitudes of others. "Alcoholics Anonymous" has developed a fine reputation for assisting the lives of alcoholics in a positive manner through a plan based on a one-day-at-a-time attitude. When one takes care of the present moment, or day, tomorrow will pretty much take care of itself.

• Keep a journal. Analyze what is being done and why. A schedule of activities will alert the individual to a train of thought that is habit forming. Reasons for and against an activity can be beneficial to sift through to clarify one's actual desires. The journal idea is something that is not often done by people who procrastinate and it is just another item that doesn't get done.

• Non-condemnation. A journal allows for frequent reviews of progress. Reprimanding oneself for not progressing is detrimental to success; rather, focus should be placed on the successes in life, taking special note of the promptness with which the tasks were handled. Self-praise should be offered and accepted in a caring way. A job well done requires acknowledgement, at least, by the accomplishing individual. Pride in one's own accomplishments, without the need to boast, is a quality for which to strive. When praise from others is desired, it is elusive, but when the seeking ends, like money, it comes around and is obvious to all.

• "Life-Directed Thinking": Guiding thoughts of a constructive nature takes constant attention. This substitution process of replacing a negative with a positive is not new, but the process must be clearly understood. It must be realized that suppressing a negative is not to be done; instead, replacing that negative with a positive is what is meant by "Life-Directed Thinking." When something is suppressed, energy is created. It is like plugging it into the wall and charging it with electricity. To eliminate procrastination, do not focus on it; rather, focus on the results of being a doer. Doers are sometimes criticized by critical people, but as a general rule, critics do not get much done, except to criticize. It is easy to be a critic, but being a doer requires effort, risk and change.[81] All change for a better world comes from within the individual. A better world begins with the individual.

Prime Time

"Prime Time" is that time during a day when one is most productive. Some people say they are morning people, while others insist they are night people. Without going into elaborate detail about individual "prime time" and the reasons behind a person's "best times," special attention is due the 24-hour cycle, or circadian rhythm,[82] that exists in every human being. Simply defined: this is a daily rhythm meaning "about a day," from the Latin: "circa dies."

In the course of a day, there is one familiar signpost of a changing physical state: the internal temperature. Body temperature varies about a degree or two, every 24 hours with almost clocklike regularity. A person's "prime time" of the day is likely to coincide with the body's highest temperature; this usually occurs in the afternoon or early evening for a person who is active by day and sleeps by night.[83] It does vary among individuals, depending upon a variety of things, such as whether a person sleeps well, is anxiety-ridden, and so forth.

"Prime time," then, is the period of greatest accomplishment, and the available time is the best time to attend to other people's needs. "Prime time" occurs when one concentrates best, or is most efficient. Select two hours each day when it appears that the greatest clear-thinking or most accomplishments take place. Once these hours are isolated, they should be used to the optimum. An unorganized person, feeling great during these hours, will sometimes be quite industrious in clearing up clutter, but will not really get anything accomplished. Through the acknowledgement of "prime time," time becomes a more useful tool and accomplishments become easier. This is one particular area where the "work smarter, not harder" phrase applies.

Time Out

Time to relax, quiet time and time to think are smart times. A balance in a working day is desirable, and rest time or break time should be as effective as possible. Everything in life seeks balance. To seek balance is to be complete. Polarity, or action and reaction, is met in every part of nature; in male and female; in positive and negative; in darkness and light; and in work and rest. This inevitable dualism is evident throughout all nature; each thing is a half and requires another part to make it a whole; i.e., as spirit, matter; subjective, objective; motion, rest.[84] Time for thought and pensive projection for positive results is most beneficial.

Habits for Success

The human being, by his very nature, is success-oriented. Failure to achieve does not intimidate, to any large degree, or demoralize the individual in his early years. A baby, for instance, while lying in the crib, will continually reach for a moving object, continuing to strike until the object is reached. When learning to walk, he falls continually — failure upon failure — but knowing, through observation, that walking is possible. Such striving continues until walking is mastered.

Habits aimed at the betterment of mankind and individual advancement may then be learned, just as they were learned from birth. Habits of personal interactions, motor skills, and yes, habits of thinking, can all be adapted toward a goal-oriented end.

This writing deals with both the forming of habits and the restructuring of old, undesirable habits. It is known that habits are formed through a process of discovery. Habits are formed by discovering a method of solving a problem; a method of achieving a process; and a method of obtaining a satisfaction. The method discovered becomes standardized, i.e., habitual — because it is satisfactory, because it works well enough, or because it is the best method available, even if it works badly.

The human being is a creature of habit. A few habits by which everyone on this planet is affected are: posture; punctuality; reading; sleeping positions;

procrastination; memory use; even certain habits of dress. A simple example is of dressing in a particular way, acceptable to those in the same locality. Likewise, in that same locality, whether realized or not, people tend to acquire an accent in their speech. An accent is acquired without practice, and by acknowledging a way of talking that is acceptable to people in a given area. When put into a situation with people from an entirely different culture, the habits of costume and of speaking — those same routine tools that gave satisfaction and reassurance and were hardly recognized — now become conspicuous and even absurd. A re-education process may be in order.

Habit formation applies also to those habits, or perhaps better, sets of habits called skills. Take, for instance, typing. Typing instructors in high school courses say there are always one or two pupils in the class who never learn at all, even though they go through all the motions. For these pupils, being able to type offers no satisfaction, not even the satisfaction of pleasing the teacher. So they just don't learn. This behavior was covered in the section on Desire.

But what of the majority of pupils who really do learn to type? Do they acquire this skill through repetition, through practice, through doing the exercises? At first sight, this may seem to be the case, but upon closer investigation, the truth can be seen. What a typist must do, above everything else, is to achieve a coordinated and well-paced rhythm at the keyboard. Little by little, a rhythmic type of movement is developed. It is not so much repetition, but rhythm; a combination of doing and feeling that is achieved. Some people are very adept at helping learners to discover the right movements and rhythm quickly and surely. With the assistance of a skilled guide, one can move through the learning process with amazing speed, saving much time and effort.

Some habits can be formed very quickly, e.g., taking sleeping pills, smoking, and other physically gratifying aids. With these, satisfaction is found almost at once. Other habits, such as typing or playing the piano, take a long time to form. The reason why skilled habits take so long to learn is not related to the amount of drill and repetition. The reason is that the precise technique is difficult to master. This may be equated with a research worker who spends years on experiments before hitting on the correct solution. There are many reasons for believing this; one of the most convincing is that a first-rate teacher or guide can significantly reduce the learning time by helping the learner to discover the right method far faster than normal.[85] In business, a management team will act as the guide. The specifics of this training technique, as applied to the employee, will be covered in a later section titled, the Personal Success Plan (PSP).

Human beings tend to follow standard ways of acting, feeling and thinking. These are their habits. To be sure, these habits were acquired as methods discovered for dealing with some type of problem, and they became standard because they worked well enough, or because no better method was available at the moment.

Habit Restructuring

Habits acquired in the "formative years" often remain through adulthood. Understanding the rea-

Acquiring Skills

sons why a particular habit has been acquired can be
a significant factor in its removal. Past experiences
and behaviors are likely to play an important role in
current relationships and environmental make-up.
Ridicule, embarrassment, condemnation, or other
emotional factors encountered as a child impact the
psyche of the individual in his adult expression. The
reverse is also true. Support, love, accolades and
other positive reinforcements during childhood can
help build an underlying base of self-confidence in
adult life. A habit always has meaning. It may be
helpful to ask a question for which the answer is not
known. Probing the mind in this manner may cause
an answer to surface. For example, use questions
like: "Why do I over-eat?" "Why am I indecisive?"
"Why do I abuse my body by not listening to its
signals for rest?" "Why am I socially uncomfortable
with others?" and "What is the reason I do not like to
take orders?" In the same vein, a statement of what is
desired is also beneficial. State what is desired,
verbally and aloud; then listen to the inner feeling
telling why that quality is not being presently
expressed. Both cases require that one be a good
listener. The fine art of listening is a talent, and like
other talents, must be cultivated.

When endeavoring to restructure a habit, an
understanding of the purpose is essential. Here, goal-
setting makes the process an easier one. Desiring to
become more efficient at tennis is an example. This
requires a fairly extensive reorganization of behavior
patterns, especially for those who have never played.
There are various rules and attitudes connected with
tennis besides the skill of hitting the ball, and all of

them must be acquired. Nevertheless, successful methods of acccomplishment are well known. Understanding the reasons for a habit is necessary, but it is not, in itself, sufficient. A direction, a goal, provides a purpose for redirection; without it, one is rendered helpless.

It is possible that an individual may be moving along in a direction that he does not fully understand, trying to achieve something, but not quite sure of what it is. When the goal is vague, it is not possible to make intelligent decisions about methods and procedures, and undesirable habits are difficult to discover at this point. This is because a habit is a tool for living; a means to an end; a standardized method of accomplishing a purpose.

Sometimes a person chooses to keep an undesirable habit, even though it is not success-directed, even though it may cost him a job, or even though others encourage him to change. The thought of functioning differently is not a viable possibility for some, simply because they have made a particular decision. This happens frequently, but the decision is made with open eyes, understanding of purpose and acceptance of the result.

The actual restructuring of a habit is brought about through intelligence. This is one of the most distinctive, fruitful and helpful ideas developed by modern psychologists in their study of the learning process. The idea is supported by a great mass of research evidence, and is widely agreed upon among experts. One may slip into an undesirable habit and be unaware of it. With proper guidance, this habit may be called to attention, and the redirection process can be implemented immediately. Thus, the key to habit control is applied intelligence.

Entire lives have been remolded out of need, such as the loss of an arm or a leg, or the need to terminate a particular type of work. Companionships, partnerships, marriages, all change continuously. Relationships that were formed on a permanent basis somehow end, only to begin again at a later date with another. Relationship-applied intelligence can change one's life; a reshaping process can take place. No one is destined to live in the past, bound to habit; change is always possible. Habits can be changed or restructured. The way toward restructuring a habit is with clarity of purpose and intelligence.

If purpose and intelligence are what is needed to restructure an unwanted habit, why, then, are New Year's resolutions so ineffective? Why do most people fail to keep even their mid-year resolutions? This is because some element is usually missing. As mentioned earlier, a plan of action is necessary. Certainly one would not expect to restructure a habit unless one had resolved to do so. But resolution alone will not do the job, any more than resolution alone will, for example, cure a cold. To state that there will be no more worry or anxiety would be futile. To say that assertiveness will replace passiveness, and that anger will be tempered, would only mean another promise. What must be done is to bring about an intelligent change in behavior, based on self-knowledge. A good resolution, plus a purposeful plan implemented with intelligence, is what is needed. Good resolutions alone won't get very far.

Habits should not be taken lightly, saying that one is more difficult to break than another. There are recognized, deeply seated habits that many possess. Still, through introspection, either instituted by oneself or by trained professionals, the means may be found to confront all challenges in life. Again, habits are tools for living. They were formed for a purpose and they exist for a purpose; they maintain themselves for a purpose, but they do not always serve that purpose well. Evidently, then, the way to restructure and improve them is through a better understanding of one's own purpose, and through a clearer understanding of himself.

Habit Strength

Many will agree that a vast number of standard ways of feeling, acting and thinking are, in reality, habits. It also appears that since they were learned, they ought to be able to be unlearned or restructured, even eliminated, if desired. However, many times an established habit seems too strong to alter.

More often than not, smoking and over-eating habits seem to master the individual. Tardiness, tactlessness and violent tempers, seem for example, too strong to be removed. These behavorial habit patterns persist, with no seeming alternative course. Those afflicted with such habits feel powerless.

Habits, however, remain only as pieces of a behavior or mode, and are built up piece-by-piece, until they appear powerful. By itself, no habit can dominate. No habit, whether new or long-established, can grip and hold any individual by its own strength; habits have no strength of their own. They are nothing but standard techniques for achieving certain purposes and satisfactions. They derive their strength entirely from the goals toward which they are directed, the satisfactions they are intended to achieve. The idea that any habit can have any strength of its own is false.

If one learns from behavior, why is it that when new skills are learned, one does not learn the mistakes rather than the successes since it is known that far more mistakes are made than successes? One may learn something the first time around, without any repetition at all. Thus, it appears that the strength of a habit is the result of the degree of satisfaction that is received. Knowing this, it is clear that one of the greatest assets is the ability to remain flexible. By remaining flexible, habits can be used as servants, rather than masters of destiny.

An example that may shed some light on this relates to an alley cat that is brought into a home. Many people have brought a stray animal of some sort into their home at one time or another. The incident may be remembered with some regret. The cat, in our example, moves about awkwardly, and darts around frantically. The situation is strange and the animal doesn't quite know how to respond. None of its habits of the wild, none of its techniques for living, work in this new environment, and there seems to be nothing that can be done about it. The poor cat cannot sit quietly for a few minutes to analyze the situation. It cannot restructure its ways to a more sensible pattern on such short notice. He has very little flexibility and, often, will not adapt.

An individual, on the other hand, is quite different. Common sense and intelligence enables him to take stock of the new situation and function accordingly. One might question what satisfactions are offered by a particular habit, decide whether it would be beneficial to change it, or continue as before. If a change is appropriate, it may be made without any undue difficulty, because habits are methods for the achievement of some specific purpose.

There is no such thing as an ingrained habit not amenable to change. The human being is flexible, probably to a higher degree than most people realize, and certainly far more than the capability is used. There are situations in which one will not cope well; the change may be too drastic, but these types of encounters are few and far between. With practical intelligence, behavior can be governed to deal with most of life's challenges.

Positive & Negative

Every habit, positive or negative, is a standard method of dealing with the problems of life; negative habits being unsatisfactory and disappointing methods, while positive ones are satisfactory and rewarding methods. Every habit, too, is learned and established discovering that it works, or at least seems to work. A negative habit is not learned out of sheer meanness or because it is basically bad, but because it really does seem to offer some rewards, even though its promises are, in fact, deceptive. On the other hand, when a positive habit is learned, one is not being especially noble, but only learning how to deal with problematic situations in an effective and legitimately promising way. Thus, positive habits can be acquired as readily as negative ones, and positive habits will grow and spread as readily as negative ones.

Habits get started because they succeed. When a new way of dealing with a situation is discovered, and it seems satisfactory or rewarding, a way of feeling, thinking and acting has been set up that has an intrinsic tendency to become habitual.

A child discovers that tantrums can be a winning card and that they are, in a peculiar sense, fun; and so the child is on the way towards a tantrum habit. A man discovers that by being a bully, other people will submit to his whims; thus the bullying habit is developed. A man and woman discover that they can talk to each other with ease and with a certain mutual exhilaration; from there, they move toward matrimony or a love affair, both of which are habits. All these instances indicate how habits stem from success.

To restructure a habit, one must clearly see that the habit to be changed is not beneficial. Usually, this is not easy. The tendencies of human nature are to rationalize, to make excuses, to attach pretty names to ugly actions, to harbor an all-embracing grudge as strength of character, to give heartless extravagance the title of friendly gaiety, and to call frivolity "cute." For those who persist in seeing themselves in a rose-colored world, there seems no hope for change. A negative habit must be recognized as negative before conscious redirection can begin.

Understanding the reason for a negative habit is a step nearer its removal. Only by determining how it came into existence, how it grew, and how it spread can the final step in the cure sequence be implemented. Substitute a good or positive habit for the negative one, then, as before, cultivate and nurture it until it also spreads, grows and gathers strength.

Achieving this process of re-education entirely unaided may not always be possible. At times, another person such as a sales manager, or some other guide may be needed, thus helping to bring to light some of the factors that require redirection. But even the most expert guides can do nothing more than aid in this process of self-re-education. Such a process can, in most cases, be brought to a successful and unaided end by the person concerned using intelligence and desire. There is no reason to believe that good habits cannot be formed and maintained just as easily and effectively as bad ones.

Action

People are judged by friends, and by their organizations, not so much by personal qualities or skills, but by actions and accomplishments. The previous pages on Focus, Goals, Organization and Habits for Success all provide useful tools to be used in both personal and business life, but they are virtually useless if not acted upon. Einstein stated that personalities are not formed by what is heard or said, but by labor and activity.[86] Even hiring decisions are soundest when blended with intuition and past experience. Individual qualities may be sought, but in the final analysis, former achievements of an individual most often tell the story; examples are past school records, work records, sales volume, achieved productivity, and so forth.

The world is filled with people who wish their success came in a neatly packaged parcel, handed over to them as a gift with no strings attached. With a few minor alterations, the Personal Success Plan (Chapter VI) offers just that, since each step in itself is not difficult. To tackle the whole is, for many, insurmountable. But by moving into action decisively, one can reach and surpass his highest aspirations!

[72]James L. Mursell, *How to Make and Break Habits* (Philadelphia, PA: J.B. Lippincott Co., 1953), p. 100.

[73]Timothy Gallwey, *The Inner Game of Tennis* (New York: Random House, 1974), p. 19.

[74]Lawrence LeShan, *How to Meditate* (New York: Bantam Books, 1975), p. 52.

[75]Thomas Troward, *The Edinburgh Lectures* (New York: Dodd, Mead & Co., 1909), p. 44.

[76]Marvin Bower, *The Will to Manage* (New York: McGraw-Hill, 1966), p. 123.

[77]Robert Townsend, *Up the Organization* (Greenwich, CN: Fawcett Crest, 1970), p. 66.

[78]Michael Le Boeuf, *Working Smart* (New York: McGraw-Hill, Co., 1979), p. 46.

[79]Alan Lakein, *How to Use Your Time Wisely* (U.S. News & World Report, January 19, 1976), p. 46.

[80]Bormann, Howell, Nichols, Shapiro, *Interpersonal Communications in the Modern Organization* (New Jersey: Prentice-Hall, Inc. 1969), p. 208.

[81]Wayne Dyer, *Your Erroneous Zones* (New York: Funk & Wagnalls, 1976), p. 180.

[82]Gay Gaer Luce, *Biological Rhythms in Human & Animal Physiology* (New York: Dover Publications Inc., 1971), p. 1.

[83]Gay Gaer Luce, *Biological Rhythms in Human & Animal Physiology* (New York: Dover Publications Inc., 1971), p. 44.

[84]Ralph Waldo Emerson, *Emerson's Essays* (New York: Thomas Y. Cornwell Co., 1926), p. 70.

[85]James L. Mursell, *How to Make and Break Habits* (New York: J.B. Lippencott Co., 1953), p. 32.

[86]Albert Einstein, *Out Of My Later Years* (New York: Philosophical Library, 1950), p.32.

VI

Personal Success Plan (PSP)

The Personal Success Plan (PSP)

Adapting to a new mental image requires both mental and physical focus. The transition into a new position or the restructuring of an old one can be effectively accomplished through the Personal Success Plan (PSP). The PSP is a guided plan of action intended to help start the transition process and bring it to a positive conclusion. The longevity of this plan depends largely on the initial implementation by the individual. Compliance with each step is suggested to ensure reliable long-term results.

The PSP considers the whole person, and is based on the premise that a wish to suceed exists in a stated endeavor, whether in the work or social environment. The PSP presents the concept that the individual is the creator, rather than the pawn, in life. It deals with the cause of success, rather than with its effects. Success begins first with the individual, and secondly with the methods of implementation. The PSP

The Personal Success Plan (PSP)

is a method of implementation, deliberately designed to help reach a specific end. There is not a single best way for all people to reach an end, but the PSP foundation is built on the premise that standard success principles, if properly implemented, will guide one through success patterns, thus ensuring the desired result. The human being is a miraculous creature. Most people, given the proper tools, can achieve higher levels than they ever dreamed possible.

The desire to learn, to change, and to take on new challenges comes from a self-actualizing tendency for life itself.[87] Life is for growth, for greater and better, for expansion and for fuller expression. This is an inbred trait within each person.[88] As stated earlier, working with another who is personally interested and involved in the success process can effectuate changes far more rapidly than working alone.

In the PSP, the reader will be asked to perform both physical and mental exercises. These exercises will entail time and concentration in specific areas and are designed to accelerate success-oriented results. The ideas are generic in nature and may be adapted to any specific situation by simply identifying the areas of concern. Suggestions will be offered, allowing the reader to elaborate on the techniques presented.

The reader is encouraged to review the Results Phase of the program, because it is the basis of the following exercises and examples.

Focus

TIME TO REVIEW RESULTS PHASE

Considering the Results Phase just read, the reader is asked to realize and evaluate his present position, carefully observing the current need status. What must be tended to are:

HEALTH_____
ATTITUDE _____
RELATIONSHIPS _____
FINANCE _____
SOCIAL ACTIVITIES _____
INTIMATE LIFE _____
BUSINESS_____

Taking stock of your surroundings will provide insight into the general trend of thought, since the mind tends to be occupied with the most current emotional impression or experience. If the impression or experience is undesirable, by giving attention to specific areas, the redirection process becomes easier. In other words, an individual must identify the areas that are robbing him of time and energy which might otherwise be spent on his desired goal. Once identified, corrective action may begin, bringing it into a more balanced state. The amount of time necessary to devote to this depressed area will depend upon its present condition. Corrective action is necessary, for if allowed to deteriorate, it will ultimately affect the overall quality of one's business . . . and life.

Many people realize the pressures of family

environment, but this will not generally interfere with the effectiveness of the PSP. Every human being can find dozens of seemingly valid reasons not to be successful. The quality of the home and/or the work environment may provide many such negative arguments. Simply stated, such overt negatives must first be recognized; then realizing that such negatives exist may make it necessary to more seriously apply the tools of the PSP to achieve Vital Enthusiasm.

The PSP also acknowledges the intrinsic intelligence of the individual. When action of any type is necessary, it will be sensed by a feeling of intuition. Many unconventional ideas can spring forth by listening to one's own thoughts. The art of listening to personal feelings requires practice and patience; cultivating this inner advice is a great asset in today's world.

For most people, the only time that is taken to really relax during a day is just prior to sleep. In fact, this has become so much the rule that in almost every case, when a person takes time to focus on total relaxation during the day, the tendency is to fall asleep. The mind can work wonders, but its effective use depends upon understanding *how* it works. Also, there are prerequisites for building individual success. One of these lies in the art of mental imagery.

A good place to begin is with mental housecleaning. This is more of an observation process than a redirection exercise, the purpose being to become acquainted with the relaxation exercise and to become familiar with focusing on the stream of consciousness. It will also allow a comfortable base for strengthening one of the most powerful tools available to the human race: the mind. When a person desires to build and tone the body muscles, he involves himself in numerous forms of physical exercise. The same holds true for someone wishing to become more mentally effective and agile. To strengthen the mind it must be stretched, pushed and pulled. The end result is not so much strength and power in the usual sense, but an increased ability to mold and shape one's inner dreams and desires into reality.

The following "Mental Exercises" will be helpful in enhancing the focusing process:

MENTAL EXERCISE NO. 2
(See appendix page 216)
THE STREAM OF CONSCIOUSNESS —
RELAXATION and STRETCHING THE MIND.

MENTAL EXERCISE NO. 3
(See appendix page 219)
DESIRED JOB STATUS.

A focused mind is a basic for success. Many people say that they know this, but the question that should be asked is: "Is this being applied?" Most people want someone to lay down a plan for success which requires no real thinking or learning, i.e., "Do this, do that," utilizing only present skills or knowl-

edge. The delusion is that they can succeed with
what they already know and the effort won't be as
great, but the payoff will still be there. No doubt, this
is a fallacy: Success arrives directly in proportion to
acquired skills, both mentally and physically. If the
general quality of life is to be advanced, then an
expanded focus must be developed to assist in the
advancement process.

Expanded focus is not so much the ability to
clearly focus the mind on specifics, but a *"feeling"*
one acquires. A feeling of: "I can handle it. I can take
on more." The stress factor is reduced, because one
becomes able to encompass a larger segment of life's
situations as a normal course of events. Self-confidence is developed. With expanded focus, one tends
to work smarter, not harder. Many people have urged
others to work smarter, but few have provided a feasible plan; even fewer have indicated the reasons for
working smarter. By working smarter, the total
standard of living is improved and the living experience, itself, is greatly enhanced.

Focus assists follow-through. When one
focuses mentally, a flow of thinking is developed
along a specific line. Just as it is known that nothing
succeeds like success, it is also true that nothing
succeeds like failure. The reason is that success or
failure will breed and build on itself. When a person
finds a constructive flow developing in a particular
area of endeavor, the tendency is to continue that
direction. People enjoy doing that which they do
well. Frequent successes develop positive reinforcement and the tendency is to enhance and build upon
them.

Personal Success Plan (PSP)

At the onset, one must begin at the beginning! To begin the task of expanded focus is a basic trait of all successful people. The building of focus can be somewhat explained through a process called "brainstorming." A person's strength of focus can be related to brainstorming, i.e., an uninterrupted thought pattern building on itself like the compound interest in a bank. The time needed for an individual to realize this phenomenon varies slightly. When thought is interrupted, the effort is increased to expand the idea. The following is a general formula consisting of four factors for developing expanded focus:

1. *Memory*

It has been said that Franklin D. Roosevelt was able to acknowledge 10,000 people by their first names. Continual reinforcement will assist in developing focus into a standard, habitual, natural pattern of thinking. A simple exercise, such as remembering names, is an excellent place to begin. Focus on the name. The first name is usually fine with most people. If the name is Robert, ask: "Do you like to be called Bob?" Repeat the name, say it mentally. Take a true interest in the other person to help build an impression in the mind. Often, people are so preoccupied with thoughts of what they are going to say next that little care is taken to direct the mental attention to the speaking party.

Memory pegs are usually not necessary if one's focus on remembering is keen. Should memory pegs be needed, Harry Lorayne's *Secrets of Mind Power*[89] provides a good basic plan: develop a mental name bank, write it down in a notebook, and make a game out of it.

Developing power of mind through memory training is just one tool for increasing the focus span. We live in a 60-minute wonder world where it seems that everything happens very rapidly. A person is born, grows up, gets married and dies all in 60-minutes on television or in 90-minutes in a feature-length film. We are taught that life is to be lived in the fast track and the picture painted is one of: "I must have it now!" There is no quarrel with the practicality of instant acquisition of possessions, such as automobiles or furniture; rather, the disagreement lies with the fact that to achieve a desired result of a more substantial nature, i.e., friends, suitable employment, etc., a constructive attitude of mind, and specific self-disciplines, such as focus, still must be acquired. The development of these attributes are attained through constant use and practice; they are not gained instantly.

2. *Vocabulary*

"If you can't communicate, you can't command!" Attracting friends, employment, and yes, even a mate, is determined largely by the use, or misuse, of language. The words that are used, the way they are used, and even the way they are spoken, are major factors in the level of an individual's success. A host of experiments indicate that when a person's vocabulary is limited, the opportunities for success decrease. It seems that by the mid-20s, the average person's vocabulary stops growing.[90] Even more surprising, diction, enunciation and usage of words are set at an earlier age.

Basic word pronounciation, or diction, is so

varied that any one language has literally thousands of acceptable variations. In the United States, definite differences in speech are evident among the deep South, New York, Texas, and California. This situation can be seen by the individual as a benefit, or looked at as a detriment, depending upon the circumstances. For instance, should one relocate for personal or employment reasons to a section of the country with a noticeable variation in speech, he might ask: "Am I comfortable with this difference, or do I wish to adjust my pattern of speech to blend with my new location?"

Speech is obviously a very personal area, thus it should be critically observed and then it should be determined whether one's present speech is acceptable for reaching a desired goal, or whether modified changes would be in order.

Regarding vocabulary, research shows that executives do not have above-average vocabularies merely because of the opportunities of the position; rather, the reverse is true. Command of the language allows one to take command.

In a study conducted at the Human Engineering Laboratory in Boston, Mass., and at the Stevens Institute of Technology in Hoboken, NJ, 100 industrial executive students were tested on vocabulary. Five years later, each person who scored in the upper 10 percent had an executive position; none who scored in the lower 25 percent had become an executive.[91]

An individual's power to learn is sharpened by an expanded vocabulary, not just in reading and language, but in seemingly unrelated skills such as

Personal Success Plan (PSP)

chemistry and math.[92] Thus, it seems that the meanings of words, as well as their use by an individual, are a prime indication of an individual's future achievements. The factors that lead to success are obvious, and vocabulary, coupled with its implementation, seems to play a major role.

Building Word Power

Acquire a small notebook with alphabetized tabs, "Word Power Notebook." Each week, with the help of a dictionary, make an entry of three words that are not generally used in your current vocabulary. The words you choose should be totally new to you or they should be words that you have heard, but with which you are basically unfamiliar.

Write the words and their definitions in your notebook. Use these words in your everyday conversations, speak them, write them, develop sentences for their use. Record them on your cassette tape for easy "drive time" reference. You need not become all-consumed with the use of these words, but develop a friendly familiarity with them.

Another device, for those who wish to carry this a bit further, is the crossword puzzle. These puzzles can be used as a mind starter in the morning. Crosswords assist not only to develop a better vocabulary, but also to stimulate one's thinking and sharpen the mind for the day's activities.

3. *Outer Image*

It has been said that the image we present to the world determines the manner in which we will be greeted. An area of focus that calls for attention, and is often ignored, is the outer image. Again, this is not meant to be interpreted as a pragmatic approach; rather, the intention is to simplify. There are no miracle cures offered here, just plain common sense suggestions — useable to all. These suggestions are:

• Receptiveness to all. First impressions are formed by feelings, as well as by visual means. Maintaining an open attitude toward all those you meet will add flexibility and resilience to your day. It is best to remain mentally open and receptive to those you come in contact with, being watchful never to place anyone in a demeaning state, either verbally or mentally.

• Visual Image. It is difficult, if not impossible, to get a second chance at a first impression. There are books, too numerous to mention, covering dress, posture, manners, and so forth in great detail. It is enough to say that a neat, orderly and clean appearance is accepted worldwide. Briefly, consider the following:

1. Wear colors and styles that are complimentary.
2. Consider the occasion and geographical location.
3. Maintain a dignified stature.
4. Keep a well-groomed head.
5. Smile.
6. Watch your language.
7. Maintain a sense of humor.
8. Keep everything in moderation, such as food and drink.

To expand slightly . . .

• Usually the colors you like and feel good

wearing are best for you. Certainly, there are variations to this, but it is a good general rule. Styles, however, tend to lock themselves in as habits. Although it is not suggested to change clothing styles with every fad, it is wise to consider updates in color and style every now and then.

Speaking of colors — in the U.S., a suntan generally indicates prosperity, health and success. However, other parts of the world differ on this issue.

• The occasion, as well as the geographic location, will largely determine what to wear. If there is a question about what to wear, a good rule of thumb is to overdress rather than underdress.

Geographic locations, temperature and seasons are an excellent indicator of proper attire. The deep South, Hawaii and the South Pacific demand that one wear something other than a Bostonian business suit.

• An individual's posture and stature are critical to success. Slumped shoulders, head hanging and open mouth (continual breathing through the mouth) are clear indications of unawareness of the principles of success. Check your walk, is it a long stride, or a short one? Do you have a clumsy walk or a graceful, light-footed walk? Note that a person's weight has not very much to do with this. The deliberateness of a person's walk is determined mentally. Keep the chin up and stand tall, just as if you owned the world!

• A good head of hair can be a real asset; so can baldness. Both can also turn the success process in reverse if not acknowledged. Clean hair seems so basic, and yet it is not as common as might be expected.

There is also nothing more obvious for a woman than a dated hairstyle. We're not talking high fashion here, just keeping up with the times is all that is really necessary. Keep in mind that the hair is to silhouette the face. Remember: you are important; whether a man or woman, your hairstyle must accentuate you!

• Smile. Of all the things you wear, your smile is the most important. How many songs can you recall where the central theme is to smile? Can you recall the words to these songs? . . . Need more be said?

• Language. Although not a visual aspect, language does paint a vivid mental picture in the minds of others. Curt, crude and cutting statements find no home in the successful person's speech patterns.

• Everthing in moderation. Again, observations by others of your eating habits (often erroneously regarded as unimportant), social drinking habits, and general moral habits are all factors to consider when designing a successful life-style.

To restate once more, these areas are keys to forming solid foundations of success.

4. *Mental Imagery*

Seeing yourself as successful is imperative prior to realizing the final physical result. With this in mind, the following "Mental Exercise" is designed to enhance and expand your own image of success.

MENTAL EXERCISE NO. 4
(See appendix page 220)
Self-Enhancement

Personal Success Plan (PSP)

7+1 Life Management Plan

Let's assume that one of your desires is to build a more positive outer image. You wish to achieve this end and you want to implement a plan for its development. Here is where the 7+1 Life Management Plan can be helpful.

1. *Write your goal down.*

I DESIRE TO CREATE A MORE POSITIVE OUTER IMAGE. Now let your mind wander. I desire to be more direct and more decisive. I'd like to make a statement; be an individual and not just one of the crowd. I would like people to think of me as: a real person, professional, stable, honest, a winner, knowledgeable, healthy, likeable, energetic, optimistic, lighthearted, helpful, caring, kind, congenial, a good sport, fun, vibrant, an action person, noncomplaining, a doer, creative, a thinker, a leader, a good listener, artistic, well-versed, a friend, aware, understanding and patient. I would like to be my own person, continually improving and having a better appreciation of the arts.

2. *Be Specific.*

Now, become more selective with these qualities you have just written. Zero in on specifics that lie within your belief system. Separate the areas and be realistic about it; but remember, for a goal to be challenging, yet within the limits of realism, you must reach out for just a little more than you think you can capture. The factor that moves so many to strive for that extra mile is wrapped in a veil of mystery, that quality of the unknown. Man cannot surpass his self-imposed limitations. A low goal is only a low self-concept expressing itself.

Your analysis might take this form: My goal of a more positive outer-image could be best accomplished by: (select only the prime areas from section No. 1).

BEING MORE DECISIVE
BECOMING AN ACTION PERSON

I would like others to perceive me as:

HONEST
PROFESSIONAL

It is important not to lock yourself into one area for accomplishing your goal since there are many ways by which your desire could come into being. You must remain open and receptive to new ideas regarding the development of your goal. In the meantime, however, it would be good to get started with a plan in which you . . .

a. Develop the habit of MAKING DECISIONS QUICKLY! Realize that both small and big decisions can be made quickly. All decisions that are made are not set in concrete. Remain flexible and open to change. There are no unimportant decisions, but for those that you really question, it is good to list the pros and cons. This doesn't require a formal declaration, just a quick list to more clearly determine in which direction you lean.

b. BECOME AN ACTION PERSON! Becoming decisive is a good base to being action-oriented. In fact, doing things NOW demands a decision. Again, develop the habit of acting on things immediately.

Make that phone call . . . NOW!
Read that letter . . . DO IT!

Buy the flowers, send them . . .
(You've been thinking about it long enough
. . . NOW DO IT!)
Begin reading that book, even if just a few
pages . . . just begin . . . NOW!
Say you're sorry. Say you're not sorry. Say
something . . . NOW!

Become an action person. NOW! NOW! Enough for
list making, it's time for doing. It all boils down to
getting your DIN degree, i.e., DO IT NOW!

    c. REMEMBER THAT HONESTY IS THE
       BEST POLICY.

Tell the truth. Sometimes it's difficult. Don't commit
yourself to do something and not follow up. Don't say
something unless you mean it. Follow your feelings.
Act surely, rapidly and truthfully and you will reap
the benefits. Above all, if you said you will do something and didn't, tell the truth when asked. It's real
easy to get caught up in a lie and almost everyone
knows the consequences of lying.

    d. TO BE THOUGHT OF AS
       PROFESSIONAL, I MUST BUILD A
       BASE OF KNOWLEDGE.

This is an area which cannot be faked.

Being a good listener is good for starters.
Vocabulary, again, will benefit in this area.
Dress professionally — There is a professional
look, i.e., tailored, classic, darker colors.
Go shopping with this in mind. Refer to
dress research.
Become an expert in your field. Even more
specifically, zero in on one particular aspect
of your job.

Personal Success Plan (PSP)

These are some very basic suggestions in being specific with your desired goal. You should certainly be able to expand on this area.

3. *Set A Date.*

Of course, there is only one time to begin anything, and that is NOW, but when do you complete it? Don't leave your goal hanging in mid-air. Set some kind of time frame, a deadline. You might determine several levels of completion. Once the completion date is set, the guidelines can be designed for its accomplishment. You might break up your three-month plan to create a more positive outer image into segments of one month each. During this time, you can design your plan to reach predetermined levels of achievement for each 30-day period.

Design a self-evaluation measure of achievement into your plan such as:

- Intentionally seek out honest feedback from your support system (those close to you). Can you stand the truth?
- Observe your circle of friends; are they changing?
- Are you feeling better about yourself as a person?
- Are you more comfortable in groups?
- Are you more sincere?
- Do you have a need to be the center of attention?
- Is your family reacting differently to you?
- Do you have more "up" days than "down" days?
- Is work more joyful and less drudgery?

Notice your growth in many areas; be observant of

the whole of your life. Ask yourself: "Am I really for someone else's success, or am I meant to be my own success?"

4. *Visualize.*

The benefits of visualization have been clearly stated in the "Results Phase." It must be clear now that the visualization process is simply a technique for impressing your desired end result in the mind as a present possiblity. Without further elaboration, it is suggested that your own visualization exercise resemble the following:

MENTAL EXERCISE NO. 5

(See appendix page 224)

VISUALIZATION EXERCISE ON
POSITIVE OUTER IMAGE

5. *List the Benefits.*

Here, let the mind wander. List all the ideas that come to you that would be considered a direct derivative of achieving your goal of A MORE POSITIVE OUTER IMAGE. You may want to list from 30 to 50 items. Clearly state: "Because of my goal I will:

> Attract more positive people
> Develop a more positive awareness of life
> Become more efficient
> Develop a healthier state of mind and body
> Become more active and less tired
> Have increased responsiveness with those I contact
> Have a revised outlook on life
> Become truly interested in others
> Become a model for others
> Have increased profits
> Expand opportunities
> Move out of my rut

Enhance my self-esteem and self-concept
Remove limiting barriers
Accept responsibility and stop blaming others
Experience a new freedom
Reduce stress
Experience an improved environment
Develop a new sense of pride
Become more mentally alert

Devote some time to this, an hour or so. This is a wonderful exercise; a tool for the mind. You will experience benefits you never knew existed.

6. *List the Detriments.*

If I don't reach my goal of DEVELOPING A MORE POSITIVE OUTER IMAGE:

She may leave me
My job may become too much to handle
The ulcer may return
I may go under financially
Stress will continue to mount
I won't feel as good about myself as I could

These are definite detriments and, although you don't want to continually meditate on them, they must at least be recognized, for we live in a world of all possibilities.

There are also detriments which can occur when your goal is reached, i.e.:

The need to move on and release the old
The trade-off for self-responsibility is the elimination of blaming others (no excuses any more)
Those who are unaware and threatened by your advancement may remark unfavorably
Reversing self-pity to a direction of action

Yes, there are many benefits and many detriments, but all must be weighed by step number seven.

7. *Make the Decision.*

For any decision to be made, someway, somehow, the pros and cons must be considered. This is done either mentally or by physically making a list. When a house is purchased, a marriage is entered into, employment is changed, or A MORE POSITIVE OUTER IMAGE is developed, the decision must be based on something. But a decision must be made. Looking at the advantages in the example of a positive outer image, it appears that they far outweigh the disadvantages. So the decison is now made:

I am creating a more positive outer image. This is becoming readily apparent to those around me.

I am becoming more decisive with each breath I take.

I am an action person; a now person.

My mind is sharp and I express the intelligence that is my birthright.

I am an honest and trustworthy person; my words can be relied upon.

I have decided that these qualities are growing in me and that they can bloom right where they are planted.

I declare this to be true; I am thankful that I am able to bring this about; and I accept it.

8. *Be Silent.*

Don't talk about it, do it! Actions, truly, speak louder than words! Sure you have a support system out there and there are things for which you might want to get some feedback. But on the whole, be quiet about it. Your goal is going to produce a positive result only if it is attained. Others know your direction in life, not by what you say, but by what you do. In the "Alanon" program for families of alcoholics, there is a statement. It reads: "Someone is following in your footsteps; are they worth following in?" Some people don't have any footsteps for they are so busy telling everyone of the great things that they are going to achieve, no time seems to be left for the actual doing.

Silence is power; it is like you're building up energy inside and saving it for a specific purpose, i.e., your goal. The author has seen creative ideas dissipated as rapidly as they were developed, simply by talking about them and not doing. As you begin to move into action, you will be able to determine where your support system really lies. Use this person, or persons, to bounce ideas off, but remember, your real strength lies within you. You are the source of your power. You are the one who makes things happen. You determine your own success. You control your own destiny.

Organization

It is so simple to become organized that most people don't take the time to do it. A janitor, housewife, engineer, accountant or corporate executive, can lighten their daily burdens with proper organization. Removing outer clutter tends to remove inner clutter. An organized balance in life at work, at play, in social activities, and in health maintenance

Personal Success Plan (PSP)

allows great forward strides, both consciously and subconsciously. For the benefit of the PSP, let's take the example of a middle-management executive. It would be beneficial to start with an overview of the tools necessary for the job.

Tools

Anything that is used to get the job done might be considered a tool, from pencils to office space, from date books to computers. With this in mind, evaluate your present needs and directions. Consider such things as:

The need for privacy
The best kinds of files
Small desk top items
Lighting
Yes, even the comfort of your chair

Also, make sure that when making a phone call and just prior to dialing, you write down the subjects you intend to cover. This way, nothing is forgotten or left to chance.

Regarding tools for play, social and health areas, a similar process may be used. What are your needs and desires? The answer will assist in determining the tools. When considering health tools, the physical area of sports equipment, workout clothing, diet and food supplements may come to mind, but don't neglect the mental aspect. Tools for sharpening the mind are as important, such as:

Visualization exercises
Memory training exercises
Relaxation
Again, diet

These are but a few items that you may wish to consider.

Surrounding yourself with the proper tools will make the job easier and more efficient. Often a reorganization can be as good as a fresh start. Disorganization breeds discontent. The proper tools will ease the mind, as well as give a positive impression to those around you.

Prioritize

A, B, C. Here is the challenge. Will you do it? For success this area demands a YES! Begin your day with the A (top priority job), not with the unimportant C. Remember to list only 10 items on your: "Things I'll Do Today" list. Begin with the A's and, if time permits, progress to the C's. This is the one area where most people fail. But you are no longer a failure, are you?

Prime Time

Again, this is an area that is best left to the reader. You, and only you, can best determine what time of day you work best. But in general, if important decisions are to be made, if a personal contact is scheduled, if an undesirable chore is to be tackled, it is often best handled in the morning hours. Fatigue makes cowards of us all.

Habits for Success

Much has been written on what makes a person

successful. This section will not deal with this area comprehensively, rather, it will condense sucessful traits, then offer suggestions regarding habit development, and finally, describe what successful people do not do. Success can become habit-forming, if one locks into the proper behavior patterns and sticks with them long enough. There are known traits of successful people, traits that assist such people to regularly outperform others. After years of testing and observation, a Berkeley Performance Psychologist, Charles Garfield, found that although high achievers tend to be a little different, generally the characteristics of successful people can be learned.[93] To begin with, top performers are not necessarily workaholics. They handle stress very well, and they are not candidates for heart attacks. They take vacations and know when to stop working. Also, they don't get bogged down in details. Listed below are six characteristics of successful people:

1. Top performers are able to transcend their previous levels of accomplishment. They avoid the comfort zone, that no-man's land where one feels too much at home. They are always striving to improve and, usually, are successful.

2. They are guided by compelling, internal goals. These goals are usually long-range and they ruthlessly work toward the completion of these goals.

3. They solve problems, rather than affix blame. All top performers learn how to recognize a problem and then organize themselves and their fellow workers to find solutions.

4. A top performer will confidently take a risk

after considering the worst possible consequences. He knows how to determine a calculated risk.

5. They are able to rehearse coming actions or events mentally. They imagine every facet and feeling of what would happen to make a presentation a success. They prepare their psyche, just as athletes mentally prepare themselves before a big game.

6. Top performers do what they do for the "art" of it and not because they are told to do a certain job, give instructions, or follow prescribed rites. They find a deep inner satisfaction in their performance and success.

Top performers are driven by goals they set for themselves. The best salesmen are good team-players who meet their sales quotas, but who also work to develop their skills. They enjoy the process, i.e., they work for the "art" of it, where less successful salesmen get their rewards from only meeting their goals, but don't necessarily enjoy the process.

Habit-Forming Through Spaced Repetition

Using constant mental bombardment to form habits is not new. This area has been used many times before, even in this presentation. The practical application, however, needs to be stressed, since through the application process stands the success of the technique. Operating on the premise that the mind can only think of one thing at a time, one can apply this premise to habit-formation with the use of a simple cassette tape player. Such devices are readily available at a nominal cost.

It may be surprising, but most people do not

Personal Success Plan (PSP)

know how to use success-oriented, motivational-type tapes. They put them in the tape player and play them like a musical movie theme. Now, good music is fine and it has its place, but that's not how to play success- or motivational-type tapes. Place the cassette into the player and listen to it for a while. Then listen to it some more. Play it over and over until it becomes familiar and you know what is coming up next. Repeat the process until boredom sets in. Play it again and again. By the end of the month, you'll feel that you wrote it, that it is yours.

Motivational tapes are developed to invoke a feeling. They are intended to conjure-up from deep within the individual thoughts, feelings and, most of all, a desire to act! When you purchase tapes of this type, adhere to this process. Spaced repetition is one way through which foreign languages are learned; a pattern is repeated over and over until finally the desired impression becomes part of the natural pattern of one's life. Cassette tapes are probably one of the easiest ways to learn anything in today's world, aside from actual experience. They force a feeling where the tendency is to act in a normal, natural and automatic manner.

Successfuls Don't Do

When seeking success, there exists a strong tendency to focus on known results; looking for the positive aspects that bring it about. As mentioned earlier, this section will deal with the reverse, i.e., what successfuls don't do.

1. They tend not to get bogged down in detail.

Most successful people are capable of capturing the general overview of a given situation. If detail is a necessary part toward accomplishment, then detail is what will be focused on; but, usually, the blinders are removed and a wider scope of vision is exercised.

2. They don't waste time. They are efficient users of the most precious commodity in the universe: time. Occasional re-evaluation is standard to ensure optimum effectiveness.

3. They don't talk about themselves and their problems. They are interested in other people, their activities, likes and dislikes. The admiration and interest shown for another adds value to a quality or possession for that person. Successful people have this interest and they express it.

4. They don't make excuses or blame others. It is always easier to blame failures on the economy, the weather, the sales team or the manager, but, in reality, these are falsely accused subjects because success begins with the individual. Successful people realize that they are the responsible party.

5. They tend not to gossip. It is difficult enough to get stories straight with first-hand information, let alone second- or third-hand garbled rumors. The wise individual does not gossip and does not put much credence in gossip.

6. They don't claim to be an expert in every field. The successful person knows his area of expertise and gives others credit for knowing theirs. They learn from others' experiences by listening and they store such knowledge for future use. They don't participate in the game of one-upmanship.

7. They don't feel uncomfortable when con-

fronted with an unfamiliar situation. They accept it as a challenge. Risk-taking is a way of life with them and, when presented with the opportunity to experience something different, they will usually opt to go for it.

8. They are not envious or jealous of the advancement of others. Self-esteem is carried high within themselves. A promotion or advancement given to others is supported by the successful person, for they know that there is plenty of room at the top. The only real difficulty in reaching the top is getting through the crowd at the bottom.

9. They are not domineering. They have no need to control others. They realize their personal and company goals and, when placed in a position of authority, they respond by getting things done. They achieve by instilling confidence, rather than by using force. Such confidence building becomes contagious among subordinates.

10. They don't criticize. They are doers, not blamers. It is common for unsuccessful people to spend a lot of time being critics, while a successful person has no time for such nonsense. They are too busy doing and achieving to spend their time on such petty matters.

These areas, if allowed to continue in negative patterns, may cause problems in achievement and non-productivity. Watch for them. Be cautious, however, not to focus on these areas in a critical fashion. Rather, the reason for alert observance is to be ready so the thinking process can be rechanneled in a more positive direction.

On the Lighter Side

Cultivating an easiness with oneself during the implementation of the PSP can make the growing process more meaningful and successful. Strain to accomplish can be substituted with desire to accomplish when humor is interjected. It is impossible for an individual to take his work too seriously, but it is quite possible for one to take it too soberly, and this is most often the case. For some reason, there seems to be a popular myth that the temptation to be humorous must be suppressed to project a dignified experience. This rests, of course, on a misconception of humor; often people think of humor as something frivolous, even a little cheap, and they are rather reserved in any such display.

True humor is difficult to define. Most people would agree that it is something deeper than mere wit or horseplay; that it carries a deeper, more sensitive connotation; that it is universal and human; and that it is a matter of attitude, rather than of things. An old joke can be dragged into a conversation and perhaps raise a laugh, yet fail utterly at being humorous. On the contrary, one may talk sincerely of serious things with a whimsical, individual twist and command the complete attention of the listening audience.

The most popular definition of humor is one which links it with a sense of incongruity. A sense of incongruity, in turn, must rest upon a sense of values, a well-balanced appreciation of the fitness of things. This is a true and rare sort of wisdom. If this seems too broad a statement, think how many wise thoughts have been expressed with a touch of humor and how many humorists have been rated as prophets. Will Rogers, Mark Twain, and Abraham Lincoln were consistent humorists; and all three were regarded as philosophers and preachers making practical contributions to society. Rogers poked fun at those in the political arena while Lincoln told ridiculously funny stories to illustrate his most determined opinions or political views. Twain, too, made pointed and thought-provoking statements utilizing humor.

Consider a group of college students at a party or in a cafeteria, notice the smiles and occasional bursts of laughter, even though they have been discussing matters that they take quite seriously. Much is to be learned from a casual approach to humor. Generally, when humor is introduced into the business realm, it is done forcefully with the intent of being humorous, but not in order to be clear, or natural, or illuminating. The result is that the humorous effort appears to be dragged out. The jokes may be funny, but they are irrelevant; they exist as jokes, for their own sake, but they interrupt the flow of thought and hinder more than they help. This is a strained type of humor that is artificial.

The kind of humor that is really worthwhile is the kind that grows naturally out of a thought; it is really part of the thought, not a piece of foreign matter. The most genuine and most effective humor is that which manifests itself not so much in humorous stories and examples, but in spontaneous twists of phraseology and flashes of imagination, and is executed in a lively sense of connotation. The reader is not encouraged to become the office jokester, but humor can be beneficial in developing a light-hearted attitude, thereby lessening job stress and tensions.

Can an individual learn to become more light-hearted? Yes! It is a question of bringing out that which is already there. Often, self-consciousness is a chief obstacle. Also, there is, on occasion, a failure to understand other people. Experience, observation and a desire to communicate will do much to remove these difficulties. Laughter has the ability to mend relationships, as well as to heal the body.

There are certain elements, however, that cut and bite into humor and can actually be detrimental to weaving secure relationships. At times, humor is used (and by some continuously) to raise oneself by supposedly lowering another. Be especially watchful of this type of humor; it is created out of low self-esteem and can be demeaning and cutting. With respect to this, some points to consider would be:

1. LAUGH WITH — NOT AT. This may seem very basic and, yet, many unsuspecting parties fall prey to this very area, especially upon entering a new business where patterns have already been set by present personnel. A pointed, pseudo-humorous attack toward an intended victim will not win friends nor will it influence people — it will only alienate. Poking fun, at another's expense, is never considered good taste. The aftermath of the folly usually leaves one feeling remorseful at his unkindness, or shameful for being involved in the distasteful pursuit. The humor that laughs with, rather than at

someone, is the kind that disarms opposition and gains support.

2. SUPPORT DIGNITY. The downfall of false dignity can be humorous, such as slap-stick versions of humor where someone is lifted from his ivory tower by absurd means; but the demise of real dignity is never amusing. True dignity is an admirable qual-ity; it is an honorable position and should be treated as such. Humor, slanted toward diminishing true dignity, will turn on itself. It is initiated only by an unaware person.

3. BE CAUTIOUS OF SARCASM. When used properly, sarcasm can make a strong point, and be made humorous. When used as a tool to undermine, however, scathing wit is not only humorless, but also unappealing. It may provoke a few ill-fated laughs, but this type of humor will not win either sympathy, approval or support.

The bottom line remains: One who has a sense of viewing life on the lighter side will find the tasks at hand easier and more enjoyable. Such ability can be cultivated through practice.

Action

The PSP, thus far, will be meaningless unless you are now motivated to become action-oriented. This means to achieve. Many things will move someone to act, e.g., fear, shame, gain, reward, and, of course, a basic motive, i.e., how ingrained is the desire or need?

Personal Success Plan (PSP)

People can always act more effectively when there are principles to guide them. Knowing what to do, they don't have to wait for instructions. And when the principles are welded together by a clearly understood system, action becomes even more purposeful and productive. To be successful, at least 90 days should be allowed for the implementation of the PSP. There will be peaks and valleys in the process, but the rule remains: Success must, by process of law, build on itself to a fruitful end.

Personal Success Plan (PSP)

[87]Carl Rogers, *On Becoming A Person* (Boston: Houghton Mifflin Co., 1961), p. 225-241.

[88]Genevieve Behrend, *Your Invisible Power* (Marina Del Rey, CA: DeVorss & Co., 1951), p. 52.

[89]Harry Lorayne, *Secrets of Mind Power* (New York: Frederick Fell, 1961).

[90]Wilfred Fund and Norman Lewis, *30 Days to a More Powerful Vocabulary* (New York: Pocket Books, 1970), p. 4.

[91]Ibid.

[92]Ibid.

[93]Western Assoc. Newsletter, *Successful People* (vol. 7, No. 5, May 1982), p. 1.

VII

The Evaluation Process

VII

The Evaluation Process

Although a strong person or firm cannot help a weaker person unless that individual is willing to be helped, this book has established that a strong support system is absolutely necessary for the PSP to be thoroughly effective. Merely from a corporate economic point of view, it would seem that this area should surely be considered. Certainly the true value of an employee cannot strictly be measured in dollars and cents. However, it is obvious that the cost and time of training a new employee, even reconditioning a present one, make the adherence to a closely supervised evaluation plan desirable.

The PSP provides an organized plan in which the individual may pursue on-the-job training with the utmost efficiency. In addition to the PSP, the individual must have available a detailed plan describing the innermost workings of his position within the organization. Unlike the PSP, which is

The Evaluation Process

generic in nature, this detailed plan will zero in on the particular position that is being pursued. It will tell that individual what to expect in the position, i.e., work schedules, people contact, job and area familiarization, and other particulars necessary to orient the individual in his new environment. Those particulars are best identified when he first joins the company.

The evaluation plan presented here is designed to create an arena for accomplishment among those seeking advancement. Many may find this plan too elementary; too simple for real life. The author disagrees. This process can be rapidly and effectively instituted in a large or small company, or even be used by an individual. If properly followed, it will be successful and will truly bring about the key objectives. The strength of this plan lies in its simplicity. In today's complex world, simplicity, clarity of purpose and action are vital factors for success. Most companies today tend to get bogged down in following plans and rules strictly from the book. This approach is often too rigid; it does not offer the flexibility necessary for the individual. An individual is an individual and must be treated as such. With this in mind, the following is presented as a blend to the PSP to assist, direct and evaluate an individual's performance.

Focus

Here, individuals try to develop an expanded state of focus; a state in which one moves confidently forward. Such endeavors produce a gradual increase in work-load capacity for employees while they concurrently experience a decrease in their general stress level. This will be accomplished in the Focus area by their attention to Memory, Vocabulary, Outer Image and Mental Imagery.

During the employee's focusing process, it is important that the employer focus on specific areas as well. Three prime areas for consideration would be those that produce results in group cohesiveness and acceptance; acceleration of the learning process; and an evaluation of the employee. Suggestions are offered here for each of these categories:

Group Cohesiveness and Acceptance

The employer should:

1. Create a group identity. When speaking of a management team, or when relating to the individual within a group, it is wise to speak in terms of "We," rather than "I" and "Me." Also, by referring to departments, as opposed to individuals, an employee can obtain an overall feeling of group identity.

2. Build a group tradition. A caring feeling carries a positive impression. Consider having an inauguration day for a new employee, something that says the company cares. Be consistent with others in the group or firm by acknowledging birthdays, weddings and the like. Even a minor celebration carries a powerful impact.

3. Stress team work. People will never work as hard for the boss as they will for the good of the team. Attribute all credit to the group to help instill the feeling of, "I can't let the group down." By prais-

ing one individual exclusively, a "star" system will result. This will tend to alienate the others and develop an "every man for himself" attitude.

4. Recognition. Be aware and be observant. Acknowledge good attitude, telephone etiquette, customer greetings, punctuality, going the extra mile, and also acknowledge individuals who promote confidence in others. A word of caution: when recognizing high-status members of a group, remember to provide a balance by recognizing low-status members as well.

5. Provide group rewards. Individual incentives are good, but they tend to promote "stars." Alternatives are to hold special affairs, dinners, present letters of commendation to the group, and offer plaques. Also, a manger will do well to reflect any reward on the group, "I could not have done it without you."

6. Stay psychologically close. For better understanding of an individual and to gain added insight into that person's work, it can be helpful to remain psychologically in tune with that person. Fighting for the team can assist in this process.

7. Treat people like people. People are not machines; they have hobbies, individual interests, families, goals and aspirations. Find out something special about the person; lift him out of the realm of computers and place him into the human arena.

Remember, an employee is busy becoming familiar with new people, surroundings and duties. In the beginning, don't expect him to focus too closely on the personal aspects of others; this will occur in due time. For now, it is well that he adheres to the PSP.

Accelerate the Learning Process

1. Memory: A simple process is to use first names, rather than titles, when discussing matters that are job related. Acknowledge employees who increase memory power and their attempts at job applications.

2. Vocabulary: Provide timely explanations of jargon; also express a true interest in the Personal Word Power Notebook. Occasionally interject a word or two from their own Word Power Notebook into a conversation.

3. Outer Image: Be a model. If one wishes others to follow, one must lead. We teach by example and the best way to teach is to be an example. A new employee will learn much by observation. He will notice the dress patterns of his peers and managers, and, as a rule, will pattern himself accordingly. To the person down the line, the president is a success. This is the position that those below are aiming at. Whatever the boss is and does becomes the qualification standard for the job he occupies. Consequently, imitation will play a very strong part in setting up the basis for management development. Positive feedback regarding dress, facial expressions and diplomatic handling of situations will always accelerate the learning process.

4. Mental Imagery: This is a personal area, though it might be well to discuss management's desired employee image. In doing so, it will enable management to provide constructive, as well as positive feedback.

5. Evaluation: Management may assist in

The Evaluation Process

guiding an employee to success by implementing periodic employee evaluations. One method is impromptu questioning. The questions are asked to determine whether areas specified for review have, in fact, been reviewed. These are often called "Hit or Knock-Out" questions. The questions will mainly deal with the details of the job, and are not really relevant to the PSP guidance system. Hit questions must not be used to embarrass or to intimidate; they are simply a means to establish where further focus is needed. When implemented in a caring and tactful manner, they can be an excellent tool for evaluation.

Focus on the critical areas of responsibility. Don't be concerned with trivia. Subordinates will put forth their best efforts in their area of responsibility when they know inspection will take place. People do best in that which is to be inspected, not in that which is expected.

Evaluation Interview

Another method to provide feedback is the evaluation interview. The interview, not the evaluation, is the heart of the evaluation process. Some firms prefer to substitute the word "evaluation" with "Appraisal," "Development Review," "Development Interview" or "Development Program." Use the phrase that best fits the understanding of those within the organization.

In preparing for an evaluation interview, review the employee's strengths and weaknesses. Don't read off the evaluation sheet. Talk to the individual in an "off the cuff" manner. Have an unhurried attitude. Pick a time when the employee's attention is not demanded elsewhere. Give notice of the interview ahead of time, but not too far ahead, for this may cause worry. Give enough time for planning, possibly a few days; this is usually ample. Do not take phone calls during the interview. Devote total attention to the employee. Keep it private. Have notes on things that should be stressed. Pick a favorable location and climate. Ask questions; this is the best way to listen. Let the employee talk! The most unfavorable climate is created bv telling stories of when *you* were starting in the c npany. Establish development plans and controls, but don't force agreement. A good evaluation interview helps the individual to accept a recommended program.

End the interview on a pleasant note with such statements as: "This has been a very valuable session for me and I hope for you also." "I feel we accomplished quite a bit and I look forward to seeing the results of our discussion." A statement of encouragement to close the meeting is a must.

There are secondary benefits to an evaluation interview. By remaining alert, one can learn how successful he is at motivating subordinates. It also provides a review of what one is trying to accomplish, and it can suggest ways to improve on-the-job results for both parties.

Goal-Setting and Organization

In assisting the employee through the various phases of the PSP, all the while providing a firm base for evaluation, group goal-setting and organization are combined. Without a plan, there is no objective. If there is no objective, then there is no reason to organize to reach it, since a destination is unknown. Planning and organization are basic elements of management and are integrated. Organization's only purpose is to reach an objective. Therefore, to be organized, one must be goal-oriented.

First, it is important to take time to inform an employee of the company goals. What is the company philosophy? What is the mode of operation? By providing this overview, along with a brief description of management personality, it will lend insight into where an employee stands; combined goals can then be examined and compatability can be established. When both the employee and the company reach their objectives, group esteem is enhanced. Goals do not have to be rational, appear immediately feasible or even be realistic. They must, however, accurately express the deepest motivation of the individual or the people in power, i.e., those who direct the destiny of a company.

Job Description

An employer's organizational duties essentially begin with an employee job description; every person is entitled to know the conditions that will exist when a job is satisfactorily performed. The job description itself has four elements. First is the objective or purpose of the job. Second, the scope of the job. Third, the delineation of responsibilities and authorities and, finally, the working relationships of the job, i.e., to whom one is to report, and in turn, who reports back. The following is a suggested format for a job description and related performance charts. Adapt it as required.

(Figure 6)

DISTRICT MANAGER
Job Description

The District Manager is generally responsible for 5 to 10 sales representatives.

During the performance appraisal, the District Manger and the Sales Manager should review this job description. They should agree on objectives consistent with the company goals and objectives and the performance required by the District Manager to meet those goals and objectives.

This job description is prepared in five sections. Section I designates the particular Functions of the District Manager. Sections II and III identify the areas of Information Exchange and Interpersonal Relationships. Section IV indicates Self-Improvement and Development methods. Section V specifies measurable Performance Standards.

I. Functions
   1. Train sales representatives in:
     a. product knowledge
     b. sales techniques and methods
     c. company policies
     d. territorial organization
     e. account management
   2. Work with the sales representatives on an individual basis at least four days each week.

3. Cover territories for sales representatives in an emergency, (not during vacation time).
4. Direct activities of sales representatives.
5. Interview sales candidates.
6. Prepare sales budgets (forecasts) with members of the district sales team.
7. Gather and organize information on competitive activity.
8. Assist sales representatives in the preparation of territorial analysis.
9. Conduct district sales meetings.
10. Assist in preparation of company-wide sales meetings.
11. Prepare sales expense budget for sales team.

II. Information Exchange
1. Submit reports on sales calls, prospect calls and competitor activity to Sales Manger.
2. Participate as a member of the Sales Management Team.
3. Recommend territorial realignments to Sales Manager.
4. Participate as a leader of the District Sales Team.

III. Interpersonal Relationships
1. Conduct sales performance review with individual sales representatives each month.
2. Counsel sales representatives and other immediate subordinates.
3. Prepare qualified subordinates for promotion.
4. Set sales objectives with sales representatives.
5. Report to Sales Manager.

6. Coordinate daily schedules of sales representatives with company specialists.
7. Participate in both company and industry trade shows and conventions.
8. Assist during company inventory.
9. Maintain sales team concept.

IV. Self-Improvement and Development
1. Conduct a personal time study twice a year.
2. Attend professional training seminars.
3. Read sales and management books and other trade publications.
4. Examine and revise this job description.
5. Write a self-evaluation twice a year.
6. Conduct an evaluation by your subordinates.
7. Attend college.

V. Performance Standards
(All or some of the Performance Standard may be applicable depending on the goals and objectives of the company. These Performance Standards represent the results of the District Sales Team.)

The Evaluation Process

	budgeted	actual	over/under
1. Sales volume	___	___	___
2. Percent gross profit	___	___	___
by sales rep	___	___	___
	___	___	___
	___	___	___
	___	___	___
	___	___	___
3. Dollars gross profit	___	___	___
by sales rep	___	___	___
	___	___	___
	___	___	___
	___	___	___
	___	___	___
4. Average number of accounts	___	___	___
5. Sales volume per account	___	___	___
monthly	___	___	___
6. Gross profit per account	___	___	___
monthly	___	___	___
yearly	___	___	___
7. Number of orders	___	___	___
monthly	___	___	___
yearly	___	___	___
8. Frequency of orders	___	___	___
9. Average order size	___	___	___
10. Accounts receivable	___	___	___
dollars	___	___	___
ratio	___	___	___
11. Average days outstanding	___	___	___
12. Accounts rec. over 30 days	___	___	___
dollars	___	___	___
ratio	___	___	___

JOB DESCRIPTION

The Evaluation Process

	budgeted	actual	over/under
13. Bad debts	___	___	___
dollars	___	___	___
ratio	___	___	___
14. Dollar gross profit by:	___	___	___
canned	___	___	___
frozen	___	___	___
meat	___	___	___
produce	___	___	___
disposables	___	___	___
detergents	___	___	___
spices, etc.	___	___	___
coffee, etc.	___	___	___
15. Percent gross profit by:	___	___	___
canned	___	___	___
frozen	___	___	___
meat	___	___	___
produce	___	___	___
disposables	___	___	___
detergents	___	___	___
spices, etc.	___	___	___
coffee, etc.	___	___	___

16. Other sales Performance Standards as may be derived from time to time.

The Evaluation Process

DISTRICT MANAGER — JOB SPECIFICATIONS

Physical

> Early riser (7 a.m.)
> Occasional 12-14 hour days
> Professional appearance

Skills

> Some accounting
> Some financial
> Drive a car
> Use a calculator
> Platform skills

Education

> High school
> 2-year college
> 4-year college
> Graduate work
> Technical training
> Professional training programs

Experience

> 10 years sales experience
> 5 years sales experience
> Sales experience in allied field
> Sales management/supervision experience in
> allied field
> Middle managment experience
> P & L responsibility

JOB DESCRIPTION

The Evaluation Process

Preliminary Appraisal

Name _____Date_____

Address_____Job_____

Phone _____

Appearance	Excellent	Good	Average	Fair	Poor
Dress					
Personal Grooming					
Physical Condition					
Speech					
Punctuality					
Manner					
Education					
Experience					
Military Service					
Personality					
Physical Surroundings					
Personal Effects, Auto, etc.					

Comments and remarks:

How contacted:

(Figure 7)

The Evaluation Process

FACTOR	INADEQUATE		FAIR		SATISFACTORY		VERY GOOD		EXCEPTIONAL	
	1	2	3	4	5	6	7	8	9	10
1 QUANTITY OF WORK The speed and consistency of output and the volume of work regularly produced.	Wastes time in talking — slow in movements — doesn't plan — makes too many excuses.		Lacks interest and mind seems to be elsewhere. Doesn't put forth effort — slow.		Consistently meets standards. Doesn't extend any effort beyond.		Frequently betters standards. Steady, regular, production on the beam.		Outstanding. Leads most others in the unit in amount of work accomplished.	
2 QUALITY OF WORK The extent to which work produced meets requirements of accuracy, thoroughness and neatness.	Undependable — does not meet our quality standards — Careless —		Frequently below standard and often needs checking and correction.		Usually meets our standards in accuracy, finish and appearance.		Seldom needs correction — has pride in accuracy and finish of work.		Exceptionally fine workmanship. Has high appearance and accuracy.	
3 DEPENDABILITY The extent to which employee can be counted on to carry out instructions, be on the job, and fulfill responsibilities.	Too unreliable to retain in job without improvement.		Dependability not fully satisfactory. Irresponsible.		Can usually be relied upon to complete his work with reasonable promptness.		Consistently reliable. Does special as well as regular assignments promptly.		Recognizes needs beyond specific work assigned. Takes emergencies in stride.	
4 JOB ATTITUDE The amount of cooperativeness, interest and enthusiasm shown in work.	Antagonistic, influences others. Keeps things in a turmoil.		Feels abused — inclined to disregard orders — impulsive — complains continually.		Follow-the-leader type — usually coopertive, diligent, industrious.		Willingly contributes extra effort and energy. Conscientious.		Highly enthusiastic, persevering. Constantly seeks additional work.	
5 ADAPTABILITY The ability to perform variety of assignments within scope of job duties.	Extremely slow to adjust to changes or to learn new duties — becomes confused easily.		Rather slow to absorb new material and adjust to changes.		"Catches on" and adjusts to changes fast enough to perform work satisfactorily.		Rather quick to absorb new material and adjust to changes.		Unusually fast to learn new duties and adjust to changed conditions.	

JOB DESCRIPTION

PERFORMANCE CHART	MINIMUM REQUIREMENTS	FALLS BELOW 1	MEETS 2	MEETS 3	MEETS 4	EXCEEDS 5	PERTINENT DATA COMMENTS OR SUGGESTIONS (Explain failure to meet minimum requirements)
1. Control of Quality or Accuracy	No. of quality errors within dept./plant average or Maintains quality standards Reasonably accurate	☐	☐	☐	☐	☐	No. Errors ____ Man Hours ____
2. Use of Machine Time (For prod. employees) or Use of Working Time (For ind. employees)	Earns 15% avg. bonus, follows instructions Avg. speed, usually busy, follows instructions	☐	☐	☐	☐	☐	Op. Avg. ____ Dept. Avg. ____
3. Job Knowledge	Meets requirements of present step in job classification covering company policies, products, methods, and standards.	☐	☐	☐	☐	☐	Job Rate ____
4. Effort	Tries to do good job	☐	☐	☐	☐	☐	
5. Cooperation	Observes Company rules Gets along with group	☐	☐	☐	☐	☐	Disciplinary Action Verbal ____ Written ____
6. Attendance (Do not count leaves of absence)	3 absences or less for six months (double for 1 year)	☐	☐	☐	☐	☐	No. Absences ____ Days Lost ____
7. Promptness	3 deductible latenesses or less for 6 months (double for 1 year)	☐	☐	☐	☐	☐	One Min. ____ Over 1 Min. ____
8. Maintenance	Reasonable care and use of equipment, tools, supplies, and work area.	☐	☐	☐	☐	☐	Neat Worker ____
9. Safety	Observes safety rules No lost-time accident	☐	☐	☐	☐	☐	Safety conscious ____

IN PROPORTION TO JOB REQUIREMENTS (Check appropriate square)

The Evaluation Process

Standards of Performance

Management means getting things accomplished through people. Being a personal leader in organizing means using more than just techniques. Whenever one delegates responsibility, commensurate authority to complete the task must also be given. Use the hands-off technique. When feedback is desired, work with and through those levels that report to the individual. Demonstrate and respect the principles of delegation to make them effective. The primary factor to remember in assisting others to be organized, or for that matter in teaching anything, is that we teach best by example.

In retrospect, four major functions of leadership have been presented in this section on The Evaluation Process: (1) establishing objectives, (2) directing the attainment of objectives through job clarification, (3) reviewing performance, and (4) seeing that problems are solved and advancements made.

The communication factor in all of these areas is critical. Be careful not to present, either by manner or words, the feeling of being one who sets objectives and reviews performance, because this can create a barrier against feedback. If one places oneself in a position of: "My job is to tell you what to do and how well you have done it," most people would hesitate to ask for clarification or for help when they face a problem.

Be available for help when there are difficulties. Create an atmosphere of openness and lend a good ear; a feeling that help can be obtained without fear of punishment.

The Evaluation Process

There are leadership situations in which it is difficult to function as a problem-solver because ego gets in the way. This is aggravated when subordinates have competence beyond that of the manager. Understandably, a leader of such a group or person may feel insecure in trying to assist others in advancement and overcoming difficulties.

A person who has trouble functioning as a guide or problem-solver because of the fear of destruction of a leader image has an unrealistic view of management. No individual can be a fountain of knowledge for all things. No person is infallible. Management does not mean having all the answers at all times. The manager needs only to help coordinate the necessary resources to acquire an answer.

VIII

Summary

Summary

From an observer's standpoint, this writing makes it clear that many people place the reason for their successes in life outside of themselves. Personal success is directly related to business success. The degree of success lies directly within the responsibility of those who are in control. Worker productivity, for instance, reflects the attitudes of management, and such attitudes surround the business with either a positive or negative atmosphere, the effects of which reach far beyond the walls of the company.

Many strive for success, measured in their own terms, but few achieve it. Success in business and in personal life is something that, on the surface, often appears to be instant. All of a sudden a person or a business has made an impact on the world, but people usually fail to realize that behind that so-called instant success lies years of focus, dedication and

Summary

discipline. With the tools offered in the Personal Success Plan (PSP), the ingredients needed to express Vital Enthusiasm are found to be rather simple — which is not to be confused with easy, which is most certainly not the case. If success were easy, then all people would be successful, all people would be financially well off, and all people would be glowing examples of health — but they are not! Thus, the need to approach this area of success with a game plan and a reliable measure for fulfillment is mandatory.

The mere fact that an enormous number of businesses are virtually "out of business" within two or three years of their inception is evidence enough that there exists a need for direction toward increased stability. The PSP allows one to investigate and evaluate various areas of personal and business life, offering guidelines for results orientation. Any emotionally stable person interested in improving himself and his business will find that the PSP, used in part or in total, offers a means for expansion and fuller expression in the direction of his desire. To illustrate:

1. Many people do not realize the need to focus attention on the business at hand, scattered thinking is the result and, consequently, outer experience follows a similar pattern. The expanded state of focus, as described within the PSP, is designed to allow one to challenge himself with higher goals and to increase activities with much the same ease as previously experienced with lesser activities and efforts.

2. Proper direction equals positive result. In

business or personal management, direction is an ingredient that cannot go unnoticed. With the 7+1 Life Management Plan presented in the PSP, the foundation for achievement can be solidly formed, and in doing so, progress can be evaluated. A clear path is designed whereby one may confidently lead himself toward his stated aims.

3. The tendency to put things off until tomorrow seems almost human nature, but it is not! It appears that most people act on minor or unimportant projects first, leaving major priority tasks for some later date. "Prime Time," "Objective Effectiveness," and "Priority Achievement" are three areas presented in the PSP that assist individuals and businesses in developing constructive organizational patterns. These keys, combined with "Success Tools," are valuable aids to organizing one's business and personal life.

4. It has been said that, "We all are creatures of habit." And this does seem to be true. However, all habits are pieces of behavior built up bit by bit. People tend to return to the known. An example is when someone attends a lecture and after a short break returns to the same seat — somehow the seat becomes his and he returns to it as he would his own home. Also noteworthy is that a physical habit takes little time to develop, and through constant usage such a learned habit becomes difficult to redirect. Thinking habits are similar in that they, too, develop firmly through constant usage. They are, however, usually not as recognizable as physical habits to the unaware person. Redirection of unwanted habits through increasing human effectiveness is the main

Summary

emphasis of the PSP.

5. Getting into action is the key to accomplishment. Without action there is no opportunity for evaluation. Interestingly enough, action actually produces the side benefit of mistakes. Mistakes are guideposts, stepping stones toward a target; without them, the final destination may not be realized. The human machine is much like a computer — what goes in must come out. However, the major difference is that a person is able to take corrective action, and through choice, redirect himself toward experiencing greater good. The expression of Vital Enthusiasm demands action of a forward movement and as a result may encourage others to progress.

This book has been for naught if it does not prompt action. No idea in the universe is of any use if not put into motion. With the implementation of the ideas presented here, the reader will achieve their own inner desires in a forthright and confident manner. For those who seek it, Vital Enthusiasm can be readily achieved.

In closing, remember the words written in an essay in the 1840s by Henry David Thoreau, "If one advances confidently, in the direction of his dreams and endeavors, to live the life that only he has imagined, he will meet with a success, unexpected, in common hours."

Appendix

MENTAL EXERCISE NO. 1
REDIRECTING A DETERIORATING
RELATIONSHIP

On occasion, whether at home or in the office, people enter our lives that bring out the worst in us. If this were to occur regularly during working hours with a co-worker, an attempt to mend the relationship by redirecting your thinking could take the following form:

Picture the person with whom you desire to eliminate conflict entering the room. Note your feelings toward this person. What do you feel is the major source of resistance? PAUSE. His attitude, behavior, apperance, or language? PAUSE. Realize that the particular irritating aspect you have identified may be viewed differently by someone else. While you may view him as overpowering and aggressive, someone else may consider him weak. Your opinion of him may be tactless and curt, still others admire his ability to get to the point. Your interpretation of this person is, in reality, your opinion, which you have every right to choose — even if it is getting in the way of life's productivity.

Mentally reverse your negative thoughts about this person. Substitute a positive for a negative. PAUSE. Be careful not to force out the negative by resisting these thoughts, but merely replace them with a more positive image. PAUSE. Imagine this person laughing with you and becoming involved in a mutually enhancing and productive activity, such as a job-related task. PAUSE. Mentally converse with this person keeping the mental conversation congenial and considerate. PAUSE.

Remember that every individual has basic needs, and that these needs must be acknowledged. Each person attempts to satisfy his own need level in his own way. Your challenge is to picture the person you are dealing with in the same manner that you wish to be thought of.

MENTAL EXERCISE NO. 2
RELAXATION AND STRETCHING THE MIND

Find a comfortable, quiet place to relax. Loosen any constrictive clothing around your neck or waist. Sit, or lie in a comfortable position making sure to uncross your arms and legs.

Breathe deeply, hold this breath momentarily, then exhale.

PAUSE.

Again, breathe deeply, hold and exhale. PAUSE. Feel the air filling your lungs with this life-giving force. Breathe in and exhale. Relax your arms and legs, let them go, let them become limp.

Roll your head from side to side, slowly and easily — gently. PAUSE.

Now, breathe deeply again and exhale. Your entire body is relaxed. Imagine a violet mist surrounding you: a clean, moist mist that is violet in color.

Breathe in this mist. It is relaxing, cleansing. This imagery also enhances your mental picturing capabilities. You can think clearly; you have command of your thoughts. PAUSE.

This exercise is purposefully simple and uncomplicated, and is designed to bend and stretch the mind by allowing your inner senses to become more actively involved in the imagery process. To strengthen the body you must exercise it in new and different ways; the same holds true with regard to the mind.

Let your mind become clear and prepare for an experience in mental sensory perception. Follow along with this exercise and remember the experience so you can expand on the process later for more specific and personal applications.

Imagine, if you will, being gently lifted into the air. A firm, secure force surrounds you and you are being carried high into the air, somewhat like a feather. You can see all around the area beneath you. What do you see? PAUSE.

Let your mind wander for a moment and re-

Appendix

place your mental picture by focusing your inner senses on a green meadow beneath you. The air is clear and fresh and you can see the lush green foliage gently being brushed by a summer breeze. As you slowly descend into the meadow, you reach out to catch some leaves from the trees as you pass them. You settle softly onto the thick, velvet-green carpet of grass.

Reach out and touch the grass. Take some in your hands and smell it, inhale the clean, fresh fragrance. PAUSE. Now, to exercise the mind even more, take note of how swiftly you can switch your attention to the seashore. You are standing on a sandy beach. Smell the salt air, hear the ocean waves breaking on the rocks. The forces of nature are everywhere — feel the cool sand beneath your feet as the warm water flows in to greet you.

Realize that your mind can take you places where you have never been. Expand your mental images whenever possible by involving your inner sense of sight, sound, touch, smell and taste. Your mind is a beautiful instrument through which you can experience the richness of life. Create your own mental images. During the day such images can help you to reduce stress, enhance relationships, and promote self-confidence in desired areas. In addition, by bending and stretching the mind in this fashion, your mind is strengthened to better weave constructive and self-fulfilling moods and attitudes.

Relax in these thoughts for a moment, then resume your prior activities.

MENTAL EXERCISE NO. 3
DESIRED JOB STATUS

Sit or lie down in a comfortable position. Close your eyes and become relaxed.

Breathe deeply through your nose and exhale through your mouth. Do this several times and allow yourself to relax. Deepen this relaxation process by whichever method works best for you. When you are in a relaxed state of mind and body, images are formed freely and easily in the mind.

Allow an image to come to mind that places you directly in the situation of your desired job status or position.

Notice yourself moving through this activity with ease and self-assurance.

Observe your surroundings. Where are you? PAUSE. What is the general feeling in the atmosphere? PAUSE. What are you wearing? PAUSE. Note the color and texture of the clothing.

Are you in a room? If so, notice the details — the color of the walls; check the wall texture. Where is the exit? PAUSE.

Notice how your surroundings are arranged. Whether indoors or outdoors, notice the items near you and their placement. PAUSE.

See if you recognize any friends or colleagues in close proximity to you.

Imagine yourself successfully involved in work-related activites.

It is a good idea to involve all your senses in this mental picturing technique. Take special note of each area, sight, sound, touch, smell and taste. Create

Appendix

and develop your own mental environment that coincides with your personal desires, aspirations and dreams. Develop and mold this pattern of thinking with your choices for success, advancement and fulfillment.

This is not a matter of make-believe, for as you picture yourself as you desire, there is nothing to prevent the corresponding physical result. Thought always tends to manifest itself in physical form, so if your thoughts are positively directed to what you desire to be, you must develop as does an acorn into an oak tree.

Relax in these thoughts for a few moments, then resume your prior activites.

MENTAL EXERCISE NO. 4
SELF-ENCHANCEMENT

Prepare yourself to relax. Uncross your arms and legs; make sure there is nothing in your lap. Find a comfortable position either lying or sitting. Right now I'd like you to focus your mind on you, just you. Relax and be comfortable. Release your mind and settle into a feeling of calmness. This exercise is designed to expand your personal mental image of success. Let yourself go, relax.

Concentrate on just this moment, experience feelings of happiness, solitude and quietness. It's good to saturate yourself with quiet time, time for thought, time relaxation, time for just being yourself, listening and being in touch with your inner self and feelings. To relax is to let all your tension go, and it becomes so much easier for your body to function in a normal, natural manner. Your mind is clear and alert and this is the time for receptivity and the development of awareness. Just relax and be comfortable.

Take a few deep breaths and exhale. Let this feeling of relaxation begin to flow outward from the center of your being prevading all space around you. You are gently cradled in a blanket of relaxation. Your body feels vibrant with the warmth of circulation. Feel a flotation sensation, so nice and easy, drifting along quietly and peacefully.

Quiet spaces in your day help you unwind your mind so that you will be able to accept new and exciting ideas. Prepare yourself now for an experience in new thought. The tools you need to develop your desired life-style are available to you all the time, but are more easily recognized in a relaxed frame of mind and body. You feel undisturbed and undistressed, not only with yourself, but also with everyone else who is in your life. Everyone is here for the same purpose, and realizing this makes it easier to communicate, not only with words, but also with feelings. It is important that we tune in and become aware of our own feelings, and also have compassion and a sense of caring that everyone experiences the same good.

Accept the fact that a clear, relaxed, open mind is of great value in areas of creativity, such as imagining yourself the way you'd like to be. Feelings will naturally follow a clear, distinct, precise picture of you in your mind. Feelings will bring your mental image into reality. You are learning to use your mind in a new and exciting manner. Throw old ideas away

MENTAL EXERCISE NO. 4   221

and let your mind be filled with excitement and expectation of a new beginning. Do not strain at understanding anything; accept these new ideas with a sense of curiosity and exploration and enjoy the adventure.

Breathe deeply and exhale — relax.

By allowing yourself to relax, new doors are opened to your inner self and the seed of desire can be planted effectively.

See yourself rising to each new day expecting adventure, joy and only good coming to you. You don't need to live in the past, or strain to live in the future. Live for the present moment, it is the eternal now.

Keep a good-natured flexibility about yourself. Rigidity often prevents newness, and newness and change is what keeps us alert. Teach yourself to be easy and natural in the company of others. Say something like, "I am now highly pleasing to myself in the presence of other people." Do you know the advice that many of the great plastic surgeons of today give their patients when they dismiss them? "Indulge yourself in only cheerful, bright thoughts and use all attitudes (such as optimism and joy) that will lift up the muscles of your face." Remember, you are your attitude.

Life is not carried on by any hit-or-miss plan; for every effect there is a definite cause. Your desire for success is that cause. Your intense desire is the key to your success. Let your desire envelop you. Hold this desire in your mind. Let it consume you, let it fill all space in your mind and feel how real this desire is for you. Realize the power of this thought form. Like a powerful current beneath the surface of the sea, this image of the new you supplies energy and wisdom. Even when you are not consciously aware, it is quietly working within you, supplying you with whatever you need to bring it into reality.

A mental picture, once implanted, works simply and easily. It is a seed planted in the garden of your mind — let it grow, and as a tomato seed must become a tomato by the very laws of nature, your thought seed of the new you will grow, and you will become the new you. The end result you desire is contained in this new idea of yourself. Give your mind a chance to work. The answer is within you, but you won't see it as long as you chase frantically about looking for it. Be calm, clear and decisive in your direction. Allow yourself the opportunity to experiment. Realize that Vital Enthusiasm can consume you, once the barriers are removed.

You create your own success through the ideas and attitudes you choose to harbor in your mind. Negative attitudes produce negative results. Positive attitudes produce positive results. As surely as the sun will rise tomorrow, the success you experience will be of your own design.

You have planted the seed for a brand new you. You have planted it at a feeling level and nothing is more powerful; let it grow; nurture it with calm expectancy, and experience the fullness that life has to offer.

Appendix

MENTAL EXERCISE NO. 5
VISUALIZATION ON
POSITIVE OUTER IMAGE

You, of course, are alive; merely observing your physical body is powerful evidence of the dynamic purposeful forces of life energy within you. Life within you, as an expression of you, has reached the place of self-conscious thinking to construct, develop and expand your own desired image. Life, in all of its aspects, is a creative activity. This creativity should be expressed through you in such a way that will allow you to become more meaningful to yourself, and as a result, your surroundings will also benefit. Creating a more positive outer image is a step toward fulfilling this creative expression. Now, don't become bogged down by what it takes to become creative. Just let it happen!

As before, find a comfortable position and relax. Breathe deeply and let your thoughts settle into calmness.

Step onto the stage of life and prepare for the role you desire. What is the role you will play? Clown or villain? Friend or foe? Failure or success? It doesn't matter what previous negatives you have held about yourself; this is a new beginning and, if you want success, you must be willing to work for it. Success can be yours no matter what your age or past experience. Mentally visualize yourself as the person you desire to be; create this image of yourself in your mind. Re-evaluate yourself. Recognize the resources that lie within you, waiting to be tapped. Instead of minimizing your present abilities, develop them. As you do, you open the door of discovery and uncover latent abilities long lying idle within you.

Imagine yourself attracting new people into your life. Realize that new friends and business acquaintances can enter your life without losing any of your present associates or friends. You have everything to gain and nothing to lose. Where would be a good place to meet these new people? At a lecture? A musical concert? A park? You must evaluate where you are most likely to meet new faces. Such places can be totally new or old stomping grounds. What is important is to consciously see all the "new" faces.

See yourself getting up in the morning with a new found vigor and zest for living. Go to work using a different route. Get a fresh perspective on your day. Imagine yourself actively interacting in a positive manner with those people in your normal, everyday life. Place yourself in the mental picture as one who looks good, feels good and is well received by his peers.

Remember, it is impossible to be successful while harboring the possibility of failure. It is impossible to prosper while continuing to dwell on lack and limitations. The realization of dreams and desires comes only through constant mental focus upon what is desired. Your positive expectations will mold your circumstances and conditions accordingly.

Say to yourself, "I expect to be successful and know that I project the ideas which reflect the level of my expectations. As I am within, so I become in my external world. I expect the perfect demonstration of this positive image because I think mainly of success and achievement. Nothing else could possibly become a reality. I am real! I am a success! I am a winner! Today and every day I have a harmonious relationship with everyone I meet. This is a reflection of the good will I bear toward them. All past differences are now removed and have been replaced with an increasing mutual understanding and endeavor."

Rest in these thoughts for a moment, then resume your previous activities.

Index

Dr. James Melton will address your organization upon request. He has also created a successful series of cassette tapes. For more information contact:

The Melton Corporation
P.O. Box 1991
Palm Springs, California 92263
(619) 323-4204